Editorial Project Manager
Eric Migliaccio

Editor in Chief
Karen J. Goldfluss, M.S. Ed.

Creative Director
Sarah M. Fournier

Cover Artist
Sarah Kim

Illustrator
Clint McKnight

Art Coordinator
Renée Mc Elwee

Imaging
Ariyanna Simien

Publisher
Mary D. Smith, M.S. Ed.

Teacher Created Resources
Rigorous READING
TCR 2977

In-Depth Guide

Bud, Not Buddy
Christopher Paul Curtis

Teacher Created Resources

Author
Karen McRae

CORRELATED TO
COMMON CORE
STANDARDS

For correlations to the Common Core State Standards, see pages 79–80 of this book or visit *http://www.teachercreated.com/standards*.

Teacher Created Resources
12621 Western Avenue
Garden Grove, CA 92841
www.teachercreated.com
ISBN: 978-1-4206-2977-4
©2017 Teacher Created Resources
Made in U.S.A.

Teacher Created Resources

TABLE OF CONTENTS

TABLE OF CONTENTS (CONT.)

+ +

INTRODUCTION

Read through today's national and/or state standards for "Reading: Literature," and you will find that the work expected of students is expressed using such academic terminology as *describe*, *determine*, *develop*, *support*, and *cite*. Requirements such as these cannot be met via the comprehension-question worksheets and culminating quizzes that have long been the staples of literature guides designed for classroom use. The primary objective of those traditional activities was to make sure that students were keeping track of what was happening in the section of the novel that they had just read. Very little rigor and synthesis was asked of students—and usually none until the entire novel was read.

From a teacher's standpoint, this style of classroom analysis misses multiple opportunities to delve deeply into the details that make a specific piece of literature a classic. From a student's standpoint, this way to reflect on literature is monotonous and inflexible, and it fails to nurture the momentum experienced when one is invested in a compelling work of art. That is why the guides in the *Rigorous Reading* series aim to do much more: they aim to transform the reading of a great novel into a journey of discovery for students.

Instead of merely asking students what happened in any given section, this resource asks questions that require closer reading and deeper analysis—questions such as, "Why did the author choose to include this information?" and "How does this information further the plot or offer more insight into the themes, characters, settings, etc.?" And instead of waiting until the end of the novel to put the pieces of the puzzle in place, students will learn to add to and alter their understanding of the novel *as they are reading it*. The various activities in this resource systematically prompt students to consider and appreciate the many ingredients the author has combined to form the novel as a whole.

A CUSTOM RESOURCE

This in-depth guide has been written specifically for Christopher Paul Curtis's *Bud, Not Buddy*. The lessons and activities have been structured and scaffolded to maximize the experience of reading and teaching this novel.

To prepare your students for their reading of *Bud, Not Buddy*, utilize the **novel information** and **pre-reading activities** included on pages 7–9 of this guide. Included in this section is information about the book and its author, along with activities designed to acclimate students to the themes and/or concepts present in the book they are about to read.

This resource provides activities that help foster comprehension and reinforce knowledge of literary elements as students read the novel. These **section activities** allow students the opportunity to process short sections of the novel individually, laying a strong foundation for their ability to engage more deeply with the chapters to come. For each section of the novel, students will complete individual and collaborative activities that encourage close reading, referencing textual evidence, and drawing their own conclusions about the text.

Additionally, this resource provides students with another avenue through which they can reflect on recurring literary elements while also connecting personally with the novel. Each student maintains his or her own **Interactive Novel Log**, using it as a way to consider and then reconsider various aspects of the novel.

Upon completion of the entire novel, students can synthesize their ideas about the novel by completing several individual and/or collaborative **post-reading activities** (pages 56–73). This section of the resource includes such larger assignments as group projects and essay prompts.

On pages 74–75, **vocabulary** lists are provided for each section of the novel, along with suggestions for ways to teach vocabulary during reading and after completing the novel.

At the end of this guide, an **answer key** is provided for activities that require specific answers, and a list identifies how each activity correlates to **standards**.

Teacher Tips

For a description of Interactive Novel Logs and how to use them in your classroom, see page 5 of this guide.

An ideal way to use this resource would be to follow the complete lesson plan given on page 6 of this guide.

The use of multiple texts can help build and extend knowledge about a theme or topic. It can also illustrate the similarities and differences in how multiple authors approach similar content or how an individual author approaches multiple novels. See the bottom of page 7 for suggestions about using this novel as part of a text set.

When teaching other novels in your classroom, consider using the specific ideas and also the general approach presented in this resource. Ask students to mine small sections of a novel for clues to theme and characterization. Examine the craft, structure, and purpose of select passages. Explore inferences and encourage connections.

This guide is designed for use in grades 4–6, and the standards correlations on pages 79–80 reflect this range. This leveling has been determined through the consideration of various educational metrics. However, teacher discretion should be used to determine if the novel and guide are appropriate for lower or higher grades, as well.

KEEPING NOVEL LOGS

Great works of literature are complex texts, and complex texts are multilayered. They enrich and reveal as they go along. Successful readers are those who "go along" with the novel, too. Interactive Novel Logs give students a place and a space to record their thoughts and observations as they journey through the book. After each section of the novel is read, students use their Interactive Novel Logs to track the introduction and development of such literary elements as plot, setting, theme, characterization, craft, and structure, while also choosing their own ways to connect the novel to their own life experiences.

Materials needed for each student:

✦ a three-ring binder or presentation folder

✦ a sheet of plain paper for the title page

✦ two or three sheets of lined paper for a Table of Contents

✦ several extra sheets of paper (both lined and plain) for student's responses to the "Ideas for Your Interactive Novel Log" prompts at the end of each section

Teacher Tip
One Interactive Novel Log can be kept for multiple novels, in which case a larger three-ring binder will be needed. If it will be used only for the activities included in this guide for *Bud, Not Buddy*, a ½-inch binder or presentation folder will be adequate.

Assembling the Interactive Novel Log:

1. On the plain paper, allow students to design and decorate their own title page. Have them write "Interactive Novel Log" and *"Bud, Not Buddy"* in the middle of the page. They should include their name and grade at the bottom.

2. Add blank lined paper for the Table of Contents. Have students write "Table of Contents" at the top. They will add to this list as they create new pages.

3. Before reading each section of the novel, photocopy and distribute new copies of the Interactive Novel Log worksheets (pages 11–19). Directions for completing these activities can be found in the "Teacher Instructions" on page 10.

4. For the final activity in each section, photocopy and distribute the "Section Log-In" page for the section. Follow the directions given. Students begin by completing a copy of the "Crystal Ball" worksheet (page 19), which asks them to predict what will happen next in the novel. Students then select one or more of the four prompts in the "Ideas for Your Interactive Novel Log" section, and they create an Interactive Novel Log page that responds to that topic.

Teacher Tip
Consider allowing your students to preview the "Ideas for Your Interactive Novel Log" prompts a day or two before they are asked to respond to them. When asking students to reflect on past experiences and articulate their personal connections to a work of art, give them the time and space they need to collect their thoughts. By allowing your students to sit with the ideas presented in these prompts, you will relieve the pressure an immediate response can cause.

5. After the class has completed the entire novel and the post-reading activities, you may have students include the "My Book Rating" worksheet (page 73) as a final entry in their Interactive Novel Logs.

COMPLETE LESSON PLAN

The following lesson plan presents a systematic way to use this entire guide in your classroom study of *Bud, Not Buddy* by Christopher Paul Curtis.

Lesson 1

+ Before students have begun reading the novel, have them complete "And the Winner Was . . ." (page 8). For this activity, students will need access to the Internet or to other sources. Monitor students' Internet usage.

+ Read "About the Author" (page 7) to the students. At this time, have a discussion with students about their expectations for the novel based on the awards the book has earned, as well as what they have learned about its author.

+ Complete the "Quick Takes on Topics" activity (page 9). Consider first gauging students' understanding and/or knowledge of the Great Depression. A brief overview of this period in U.S. history may be necessary.

+ Introduce the concept of Interactive Novel Logs (see page 5). Prepare a blank notebook for each student or allow students to prepare their own.

Lesson 2

+ Read Chapters 1–4 of *Bud, Not Buddy*.

+ See "Section I Teacher Instructions" (page 20). Have students add to their Novel Logs before completing the other Section I activities.

Lesson 3

+ Read Chapters 5–8 of *Bud, Not Buddy*.

+ See "Section II Teacher Instructions" (page 27). Have students add to their Novel Logs before completing the other Section II activities.

Lesson 4

+ Read Chapters 9–12 of *Bud, Not Buddy*.

+ See "Section III Teacher Instructions" (page 35). Have students add to their Novel Logs before completing the other Section III activities.

Lesson 5

+ Read Chapters 13–15 of *Bud, Not Buddy*.

+ See "Section IV Teacher Instructions" (page 43). Have students add to their Novel Logs before completing the other Section IV activities.

Lesson 6

+ Read Chapters 16–19 of *Bud, Not Buddy*.

+ See "Section V Teacher Instructions" (page 49). Have students add to their Novel Logs before completing the other Section V activities.

Lesson 7

+ Consult "Teacher Instructions" (page 56) for descriptions of Post-Reading Activities. Synthesize understanding with the "Add It Up" worksheets (pages 57–59).

+ Choose and analyze important scenes from the novel (pages 60–61).

+ Complete larger-scale individual (pages 64–65, 68–69) and collaborative (pages 63, 70–71) projects.

+ Reimagine the text with "A New Point of View" (page 62), "Considering Genre" (page 66), and "Considering Voice" (page 67).

+ Share final thoughts and opinions on the novel (pages 72–73).

+ Consider additional vocabulary-based activities (pages 74–75).

NOVEL INFORMATION

Book Summary

Set in Michigan during the days of the Great Depression, *Bud, Not Buddy* tells the story of 10-year-old Bud Calloway, an orphan who at times displays a wisdom beyond his years — and at other times, reveals the immaturity of an impulsive child with a wild imagination. In a time when and a place where just about everyone has it tough, Bud has developed a set of rules to live by that help him survive and adapt to the harshest realities. Bud also carries around with him a suitcase filled with an odd assortment of items that seemed to mean something to his deceased mother. It's his belief that this collection of clues reveals the answer to a family secret and a destiny greater than his current fate.

This Newbery Medal-winning novel follows Bud on his zigzag quest to meet a mysterious musician who he feels must be his father. His adventures take him from the cruelty of an abusive foster family to an unexpected kindness in a food line to a night in a makeshift town where everyone has a sad story to share. Bud learns what his mother meant when she told him that every door that closes leads to another that opens, and his fortunes are forever changed with the help of a stranger passing by in the night. Ultimately, Bud is delivered to a place he never could have imagined and to a family he never knew he could have. For the first time since his mother died, Bud finds a place where he belongs.

About the Author

Christopher Paul Curtis grew up in Flint, Michigan, and he has set many of his novels in this city. Curtis spent his early adult life working on an assembly line, hanging doors on cars in a Flint automobile factory. In his spare time he wrote, and in 1996 he was able to publish his first novel: *The Watsons Go to Birmingham — 1963*. This novel earned Curtis immediate acclaim, as it was named a Newbery Honor Book and the winner of the Coretta Scott King Book Award. He would go on to write several beloved children's novels, the most decorated of which have been 1999's *Bud, Not Buddy* (winner of the Newbery Medal and Coretta Scott King Book Award) and 2007's *Elijah of Buxton* (named a Newbery Honor Book and winner of the Coretta Scott King Book Award). In his novels, Curtis often infuses warmth and humor into his portrayal of dark, difficult times in U.S. history.

Make It a Text Set!

The following novels can form ideal text sets with *Bud, Not Buddy*. (**Note:** Check books in advance to ensure they are appropriate for your students.)

Other Books by Christopher Paul Curtis	Books by Other Authors
The Watsons Go to Birmingham – 1963 (1996)	*Roll of Thunder, Hear My Cry* by Mildred D. Taylor
Bucking the Sarge (2004)	*Out of the Dust* by Karen Hesse
Elijah of Buxton (2007)	*Esperanza Rising* by Pam Muñoz Ryan
The Mighty Miss Malone (2012)	*A Year Down Yonder* by Richard Peck

NAME: _____

AND THE WINNER WAS . . .

You are about to read a novel named *Bud, Not Buddy*. This novel has won two of the most prestigious awards a novel could possibly win: the Newbery Medal and the Coretta Scott King Book Award.

Use the Internet or other sources to research information about these two important awards. Complete the chart below.

The Awards ➞	Newbery Medal	Coretta Scott King Book Award
Who is this award named after?		
Provide some information about this person.		
Write about this award. For what reason(s) does an author receive it? In what year was it first awarded?		
What does this award look like?* Describe its shape, the images on it, etc.		
In what year did *Bud, Not Buddy* win this award?		
Have you read any other books that have won this award? If so, name a few.		

* These awards' seals can most likely be found on the cover of your copy of *Bud, Not Buddy*. If they are not there, conduct an Internet image search for "image Newbery Medal" or "image Coretta Scott King award."

NAME: _____

QUICK TAKES ON TOPICS

Each reader begins a book with his or her own ideas, opinions, and knowledge. The book you are about to read explores many ideas and topics. For each of the topics listed below, write a little about the knowledge and opinions you are bringing with you as you begin the journey of reading *Bud, Not Buddy*.

+ +

Topic #1

The Great Depression

What does this mean to you or make you think of? Do you have any opinions about books based during this time period in U.S. history?

_____
_____
_____
_____
_____

+ +

Topic #2

your family history

What does this mean to you or make you think of? Do you have any opinions about books based on characters who are trying to learn about their family's past?

_____
_____
_____
_____
_____

+ +

Topic #3

the lives of musicians

What does this mean to you or make you think of? Do you have any opinions about books that show the behind-the-scenes lives of entertainers and performers?

_____
_____
_____
_____
_____

TEACHER INSTRUCTIONS

As students read through *Bud, Not Buddy,* have them use the following activities to track the growth and development of certain literary elements. For each activity:

✦ Distribute a fresh copy to students after each section is read.

✦ Have students include these completed worksheets in their Interactive Novel Logs. See page 5 for more information.

✦ ✦

Activity: "The Summaries of Its Parts"   **Page #:** 11
Focus: Plot   **Learning Type:** Individual
Description: Summarize the major plot points of the section just read. Give titles to two of the section's chapters.

Activity: "Two Sides of Bud"   **Page #:** 12
Focus: Characterization   **Learning Type:** Individual
Description: Search for examples of both Bud's wisdom and his inexperience.

Activity: "Rules and Things"   **Page #:** 13
Focus: Characterization, Plot, Theme   **Learning Type:** Individual
Description: Highlight one of Bud's rules for life. Paraphrase the rule and show how it fits into the storyline. Determine why Bud might have come up with this rule.

Activity: "A Look Inside"   **Page #:** 14
Focus: Symbolism, Plot   **Learning Type:** Individual
Description: Describe the role of Bud's suitcase in this section of the novel.

Activity: "Checking In on Theme"   **Page #:** 15
Focus: Theme   **Learning Type:** Individual
Description: Use evidence to support a claim about the importance of a particular theme.

Activity: "Making the Mood"   **Page #:** 16
Focus: Mood, Craft   **Learning Type:** Individual
Description: Determine how the author combines literary elements to create the mood of a chosen scene.

Activity: "Another Voice"   **Page #:** 17
Focus: Voice, Characterization   **Learning Type:** Individual
Description: Rewrite a scene from the chapter, but this time in the voice (and from the perspective) of a character other than Bud. Defend writing with evidence from the novel.

Activity: "Choice Words"   **Page #:** 18
Focus: Vocabulary   **Learning Type:** Individual
Description: Use context to determine a word's meaning and part of speech. Use the word in a new sentence and illustrate it's meaning. (**TIP:** Select vocabulary words from the "Novel Vocabulary" lists on page 75.)

Activity: "Crystal Ball"   **Page #:** 19
Focus: Plot, Characterization   **Learning Type:** Individual
Description: Make a prediction about where the novel's plot will go next and/or what will further be revealed about the novel's main character. (**TIP:** This page should be completed as a part of the "Log-In" activity that concludes each section.)

THE SUMMARIES OF ITS PARTS

As you finish reading each section of *Bud, Not Buddy*, take a few minutes to summarize the events that have taken place. Use the following tips to guide you.

Tips for Writing Summaries

✦ **Focus only on the most important events.** Do not include extra details or examples. A summary should be like an outline of only the major plot points.

✦ **Use your own words.** Do not quote words directly from the novel or use the novel's vocabulary.

✦ **Use transition words.** Words and phrases like *first*, *then*, *next*, and *after that* quickly show the sequence in which events occur in the novel.

Fit your summary on the lines provided below.

✦ ✦

Summary for Section #: _____   **Chapters in this section:** _____

Page numbers in this section: *from page* _____ *to page* _____

✦ ✦

_____

_____

_____

_____

_____

_____

_____

Choose two chapters from this section. Give a title to each chapter. Explain each title.

#	Your Title	Why This Is a Good Title

NAME: _____

TWO SIDES OF BUD

Bud is only 10 years old, but he has lost a lot and learned a lot in his young life. This has made him very "street-smart" in some ways. Through his experiences, he has gained wisdom and learned how to survive and adapt. But he is still very young, and he has some of the same thoughts and fears that anyone his age might have.

Think about the section you have just read. Find as many examples as you can of times when Bud acts older or wiser than the average 10-year-old. Also find examples of Bud acting very young, like any 10-year-old might act.

+ +

Section #: _____   **Chapters in this section:** *from* _____ *to* _____

Page numbers in this section: *from page* _____ *to page* _____

+ +

One Side	Another Side
Description: ✦ street-smart ✦ wise beyond his years	**Description:** ✦ young, immature ✦ thinks/acts like a child
Examples: _____ _____ _____ _____ _____	**Examples:** _____ _____ _____ _____ _____

In this section, would you say Bud acts more like a child or more like someone who is much older? Use details, examples, or quotes from the section to support your answer.

_____

_____

_____

_____

_____

_____

RULES AND THINGS

Throughout the novel, Bud tells us his rules for life. What exactly does he call them? In the box below, write the exact name he gives to his rules. Decorate the sign any way you like.

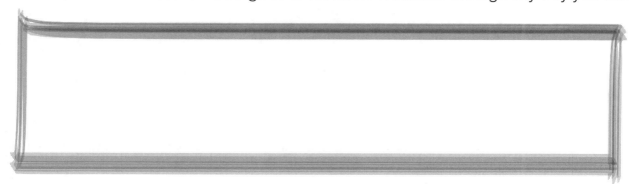

Next, highlight one "Rule and Thing" from the section you have just read.

What is the number of the rule? _____ On what page did you find this rule? _____

What is happening in the novel when Bud mentions this rule?

_____

_____

_____

In your own words, what does the rule say?

_____

_____

_____

Does this rule help Bud have a "funner" life or make a better liar out of himself?

- If Yes, then how does it do one or both of these things?
- If No, then why do you think Bud created this rule and how does it help him?

_____

_____

_____

_____

_____

_____

NAME: _____

A LOOK INSIDE

As we read *Bud, Not Buddy*, we follow along closely to the novel's main character. Something else seems to follow Bud closely, too: his suitcase. Take a look inside Bud's suitcase to see what each section of the novel reveals about its contents.

✦ ✦

Section #: _____   **Chapters in this section:** *from* _____ *to* _____

Page numbers in this section: *from page* _____ *to page* _____

✦ ✦

In this section of the novel, what happens to the suitcase? Write a brief summary of where the suitcase is during this section and if it is with anyone other than Bud.

_____

_____

_____

In this section of the novel, what do we learn about the objects inside the suitcase? Begin by naming all of the objects the book tells us are in the suitcase.

_____

_____

_____

Next, describe two of the objects in greater detail. Complete the chart below. If you don't think the book has given you enough information yet to fill out the third column, then take a guess as to why Bud keeps this object in his suitcase.

Name of Object(s)	Description	Why It's Important to Bud

Finally, in this section, find a quote that illustrates Bud's feeling about the suitcase.

Quote: _____

_____ Found on page number: _____

Why I chose this quote: _____

_____

CHECKING IN ON THEME

Bud, Not Buddy is full of themes that appear and reappear throughout its chapters. A theme is an important message behind the story.

Look at the list of themes below. Choose one that you think is very important to this section. Put a checkmark in the box beside that theme.

✦ ✦

Section #: _____   **Chapters in this section:** *from _____ to _____*

Page numbers in this section: *from page _____ to page _____*

✦ ✦

Themes

❑ **Compassion** (helping others in need)

❑ **Family** (the people who support you)

❑ **Fear** (being afraid of what is out there)

❑ **Home** (finding a place to live and be safe)

❑ **Lies** (making up stories in order to get what you want or need)

❑ **Perseverance** (never quitting despite the troubles you face)

❑ **Poverty** (facing the challenges of having little money, food, shelter, etc.)

❑ **Race** (the African-American experience during this time in U.S. history)

❑ **Wisdom** (your words/actions matter and affect others)

Why do you think this theme is important in this section? Write a paragraph in which you explain your choice. Use at least two examples from the section.

Challenge Yourself

For each section, choose a theme that you have not written about yet!

_____

_____

_____

_____

_____

_____

_____

_____

_____

_____

NAME: _____

MAKING THE MOOD

Authors have many ways of creating a feeling or mood. Think about the scenes in this section of the novel. Choose one that was filled with mood. In other words, choose a scene that made you laugh or made you feel anxious, excited, or any other emotion.

+ +

This scene is from Chapter _____. In this scene, the following events happen:

_____

_____

The mood, or main feeling, conveyed in this scene is

_____

Complete the chart below. The column on the left lists five elements the author combined to create this scene. For each element, explain how it contributed to the mood of the scene.

Element	How It "Made" the Mood
Plot (the events that happen)	
Setting (the time when and place where the events happen)	
Characterization (the people and animals in the story)	
Voice (the tone of the narrator who is telling the story)	
Dialogue (the words spoken by the characters)	

ANOTHER VOICE

All of the events that take place in *Bud, Not Buddy* are told to us from the perspective of one character (whose name is Bud, not Buddy). In each section of the novel, we meet other characters who have interesting personalities and would probably have very interesting perspectives on the events of the novel.

Choose a character — not Bud — who is featured in this section of the novel. Also choose a scene. Write part of that scene, but this time from the new character's perspective. Use the pronoun "I" when you write. Pretend you are that character.

+ +

Character's Name: _____   **from Chapter:** _____

Scene: _____

+ +

_____

_____

_____

_____

_____

_____

_____

_____

_____

_____

_____

What clues from the book did you use to determine the "sound" of this character's voice?

_____

_____

_____

_____

NAME: _____

CHOICE WORDS

+ +

Word from *Bud, Not Buddy*: _____

+ +

1. Find one quotation in which this word appears in the novel. Write it in the box.

> *Found on page _____*

2. Reread the paragraph or part of the novel that contains the choice word. Consider what is happening in the story and how the author uses the word. Based on the words and ideas around the choice word, what do you think it means?

   _____

   _____

3. Now look up the word in the dictionary and write down the definition of this word that best fits the way it is used in the novel.

   _____

   _____

4. Does the word have other meanings that are different from how it is used in the novel? If so, list those meanings here.

   _____

   _____

5. What is the part of speech of the word as it is used in the novel? _____

6. Next, write two synonyms and two antonyms of the word as it is used in the novel.

   Synonyms: _____   Antonyms: _____

   _____   _____

7. Write your own sentence that uses the vocabulary word.

   _____

   _____

8. What images or pictures does this word bring to your mind? On the back of this paper, draw a picture or diagram that you feel illustrates the word in some way.

CRYSTAL BALL

Once you have read each section, think about the characterization and the plot points that were introduced or explored further in those chapters. Make two predictions based on what you have read so far.

After each section, write your thoughts about the following questions:

✦ Where will the story go next?

✦ What more will we learn about Bud and the people he encounters?

✦ ✦

I have just finished Chapter _____ of the novel. I am now on page _____ .

1st Prediction

I predict this will happen: _____

_____

_____

_____

Here is why I predict this: _____

_____

_____

_____

2nd Prediction

I predict this will happen: _____

_____

_____

_____

Here is why I predict this: _____

_____

_____

_____

TEACHER INSTRUCTIONS

Section Note: Read Chapters 1–4 of the novel. In this first section of *Bud, Not Buddy*, we meet Bud and learn a little bit about his past, present, and future in Depression-era Flint, Michigan.

After your students have read Chapters 1–4, have them begin their analyses of this section of the novel by completing the Interactive Novel Log activities on pages 11–18. Consult the "Teacher Instructions" on page 10 and distribute copies of the following:

✦ **"The Summaries of Its Parts"** (page 11)
✦ **"Two Sides of Bud"** (page 12)
✦ **"Rules and Things"** (page 13)
✦ **"A Look Inside"** (page 14)

✦ **"Checking In on Theme"** (page 15)
✦ **"Making the Mood"** (page 16)
✦ **"Another Voice"** (page 17)
✦ **"Choice Words"** (page 18)

✦ ✦

Students will then further examine this section through the following worksheets:

Activity: "In the Beginning"　　　　　　　　**Page #:** 21
Focus: Plot, Characterization, Craft　　　　　**Learning Type:** Individual
Description: Think about the way the novel begins and what we learn about the novel's narrator. Examine the author's use of repetition.

Activity: "Getting to Know Bud"　　　　　　　**Page #:** 22
Focus: Characterization, Conflict　　　　　　**Learning Type:** Individual
Description: Examine Bud as a character. Determine what is important to him, how he deals with conflict, and how he adapts to his environment. Choose a word to describe Bud, and then defend your choice.

Activity: "Storyboarding a Scene"　　　　　　**Page #:** 23
Focus: Plot, Characterization　　　　　　　**Learning Type:** Individual
Description: Use a storyboard format to visually represent an exciting scene from this section. Determine what Bud's thoughts and actions during this scene tell us about him.

Activity: "The Last Laugh"　　　　　　　　　**Page #:** 24
Focus: Plot, Characterization　　　　　　　**Learning Type:** Individual
Description: Describe the steps of Bud's plan for revenge. Decide what his plan – and his thoughts as he goes about following it – say about Bud as a character.

Activity: "Talking About Revenge"　　　　　　**Page #:** 25
Focus: Plot, Characterization, Craft　　　　　**Learning Type:** Collaborative
Description: With a partner, discuss how the author creates expectations for the reader. Determine how an alternate outcome would affect the reader and the novel as a whole. Summarize discussions.

Activity: "Section I Log-In"　　　　　　　　　**Page #:** 26
Focus: Plot, etc.　　　　　　　　　　　　**Learning Type:** Individual
Description: Complete "Crystal Ball" worksheets in order to predict future events in the novel. Then choose from several options to add to Interactive Novel Logs.

NAME: _____

IN THE BEGINNING

How does *Bud, Not Buddy* begin? Take a close look at Chapter 1.

1. What is the first sentence of the chapter?

_____

2. In this chapter, the author gives us a lot of information about Bud. Complete the form below to show what we learn.

> **Name:** *Bud*   **Age:** _____
>
> **What do we learn about Bud's . . .**
>
> ◆ **Present** (where he is and what he is doing as the novel begins): _____
>
> _____
>
> _____
>
> _____
>
> ◆ **Past** (what has happened to him before the novel begins): _____
>
> _____
>
> _____
>
> _____
>
> ◆ **Future** (where he will soon be going): _____
>
> _____
>
> _____
>
> _____

3. What is the last sentence of the chapter? Where have you seen this sentence before?

_____

_____

The author must be repeating this line for a reason. What do you think is his reason for doing this? What do you think he wants us to know about Bud?

_____

_____

NAME: _____

GETTING TO KNOW BUD

In Chapter 2, we learn a lot about Bud through his thoughts and actions. Look back at that chapter as you answer the following questions.

1. What are some people, things, and/or ideas that are important to Bud?

_____

_____

_____

How does the author show us or tell us this in Chapter 2? Provide an example.

_____

_____

2. How would you describe the way Bud deals with conflict?

_____

_____

How does the author show us or tell us this in Chapter 2? Provide an example.

_____

_____

3. Bud has lived in orphanages and foster homes for a while now. How has he adapted to this kind of a life? Give an example that shows this.

_____

_____

_____

_____

4. In your opinion, which of the following words best describes Bud in Chapter 2? Circle your choice, and explain it on the lines below.

angry   **brave**   **foolish**   **resourceful**   **tough**   **wise**

_____

_____

_____

_____

NAME: _____

STORYBOARDING A SCENE

In Chapter 3, Bud finds himself locked inside the Amos' shed. The dark, the contents of the shed, and the contents of Bud's imagination combine to create a memorable scene.

Create a storyboard to show this scene. To do this, draw pictures of six key moments from Chapter 3. You may use a few words in each, but try to tell the story of the scene mostly through images.

1.	2.	3.
4.	5.	6.

+ +

Considering Characterization: What do you think this scene reveals about Bud? What does it show us about how he looks at and approaches obstacles in his life?

_____

_____

NAME: _____

THE LAST LAUGH

For this activity, look back at Chapter 4 of *Bud, Not Buddy*.

1. Once Bud escapes the shed, what is his plan to get revenge? Name four steps of his plan. Describe each step and explain the reason why Bud included it in his plan. In the left column, use a transition word to show the order in which he did each step. The first transition word is written for you.

Order	What Bud Did	Why Bud Did It
First		

2. Which part of the plan doesn't work at first? How does he change his plan to make up for this?

   _____

   _____

3. How does this plan help him get revenge on both Todd Amos and his mother? Write two sentences. In the first one, state how the plan helps him get revenge against Todd. In the second, state how it helps him get revenge against Mrs. Amos.

   _____

   _____

   _____

4. What does Bud say is his favorite saying in the whole world? Quote it here:

   _____

5. Think about Bud's favorite saying and also about the way he chooses to get revenge. What do you think these things say about Bud? Explain.

   _____

   _____

   _____

NAME(S): _____

TALKING ABOUT REVENGE

For this activity, work with a partner. With your partner, share your thoughts about Bud's ideas and actions at the end of Chapter 3 and the beginning of Chapter 4.

1. When you first read the end of Chapter 3 and the beginning of Chapter 4, what did you think Bud was planning to do with the shotgun? Fill out this chart.

What You Thought Bud Might Do	Clues That Made You Think This

2. How would your feelings toward Bud and/or the book have changed if Bud had shot any or all of the Amoses? In your opinion, would this act of shooting have fit the mood of the book? Discuss these ideas. Write a quick summary of your discussion.

_____

_____

_____

_____

3. Why do you think the author might have wanted you to get the wrong idea about Bud's plan? What effect do you think he was going for? Discuss these ideas. Write a quick summary of your discussion.

_____

_____

_____

_____

4. How do Bud's actions in Chapter 4 make you feel about him as a character? Do you like him more or less because of these things? Discuss these questions. Do you and your partner both feel the same way? Explain.

_____

_____

_____

_____

NAME: _____

SECTION I LOG-IN

Now that you have finished this section of *Bud, Not Buddy*, take some time to add to your Interactive Novel Logs.

+ **First, make a prediction about what will happen next in the novel.**

   Use your "Crystal Ball" worksheet (page 19) to do this.

+ **Next, make a more personal connection to what you have read.**

   Choose one of the suggestions below and use it to fill a page in your Interactive Novel Log. Take this opportunity to connect with the novel in a way that appeals to you.

+ +

Ideas for Your Interactive Novel Log

1
The Roughest Age

In Chapter 1, Bud says that six is a really rough age because that is when adults begin to look at you differently. Do you agree with Bud? Or is there another age that you think is tougher? In the middle of your page, write the number of what you think is the roughest age. (It could be an age you haven't reached yet.) Around the number, give reasons for your choice.

2
Coming A-Loose

In Chapter 1, Bud also says six is scary because that is when "your teeth start coming a-loose in your mouth." Think back to the time when you lost your first tooth. Was it scary? Did you know what was happening? Write about your experience. Or instead, you could compare your experience to Bud's. Why might your first loose tooth not have been as scary to you as it was to Bud?

3
Bugs' Story

In Chapter 3, Bud remembers the story of his friend Bugs and the cockroach that crawled inside his ear. How did that story make you feel as you read it? Did it make you laugh? Did it make you cringe? Did you imagine yourself in Bugs' situation? Write your thoughts about this part of the story.

4
Leave a Note

Imagine if Bud had taken the time to write and leave a note for the Amos family. What would it say? Write a short note in Bud's voice. Use the words and sayings he might use if he wrote such a note. In your note, refer to things that happened or things that were said in Chapters 1–4.

Dear Amoses,

TEACHER INSTRUCTIONS

Section Note: Read Chapters 5–8 of the novel. In this section, people do what they can to take care of themselves and each other in these tough times. Bud spends an eventful night in a makeshift town.

After your students have read Chapters 5–8, have them begin their analyses of this section of the novel by completing the Interactive Novel Log activities on pages 11–18. Consult the "Teacher Instructions" on page 10 and distribute new copies of the following:

✦ **"The Summaries of Its Parts"** (page 11)
✦ **"Two Sides of Bud"** (page 12)
✦ **"Rules and Things"** (page 13)
✦ **"A Look Inside"** (page 14)

✦ **"Checking In on Theme"** (page 15)
✦ **"Making the Mood"** (page 16)
✦ **"Another Voice"** (page 17)
✦ **"Choice Words"** (page 18)

✦ ✦

Students will then further examine this section through the following worksheets:

Activity: "Things About Momma"
Focus: Characterization
Page #: 28
Learning Type: Individual
Description: Describe the way Bud's mother acted and the things she often told her son. Use evidence from the novel to support answers.

Activity: "Picturing Momma"
Focus: Characterization, Plot
Page #: 29
Learning Type: Individual
Description: Draw and describe the main elements of Bud's photo of his mother.

Activity: "The Pretend Family"
Focus: Plot, Characterization, Tone
Page #: 30
Learning Type: Individual
Description: Analyze the scene at the mission. Compare Bud's pretend family to his most recent foster family. Consider the author's tone toward the family at the mission.

Activity: "Signs of the Times"
Focus: Setting, Plot, Point of View
Page #: 31
Learning Type: Individual
Description: Think about the signs outside and inside the mission. Consider how the people in this time and in this situation would view these signs.

Activity: "A Sense of Place"
Focus: Setting, Craft
Page #: 32
Learning Type: Collaborative
Description: With a partner, examine the settings of Chapters 7 and 8. Determine how the author uses sensory words to make these settings come alive for the reader.

Activity: "A Night in Hooverville"
Focus: Plot, Characterization, Setting
Page #: 33
Learning Type: Individual
Description: Describe the events that take place during Bud's stay in a makeshift town. Use evidence to show why these people are in this town and how they feel about it.

Activity: "Section II Log-In"
Focus: Plot, etc.
Page #: 34
Learning Type: Individual
Description: Complete "Crystal Ball" worksheets in order to predict future events in the novel. Then choose from several options to add to Interactive Novel Logs.

NAME: _____

THINGS ABOUT MOMMA

In Chapter 5, Bud tells us about his mother.

1. How does Bud describe the way his mother moved and acted most of the time? Find a quote that shows this description.

_____

_____

_____

2. How does Bud describe the way his mother acted when she was telling him something important?

_____

_____

_____

3. What important things did she tell Bud? Bud says there were four things she told him over and over again. Name those four things.   Give details to show what she said about each one.

Things	Details

4. How do you think Bud's mother felt about him?

_____

_____

Find a quote that supports your answer. _____

_____

_____ From page number(s): _____

PICTURING MOMMA

One of Bud's prized possessions is a picture of his mother as a child. In the frame below, illustrate this picture. Use the information given in the novel to include as many details as possible in the picture. Alongside the picture, describe five of the details you included.

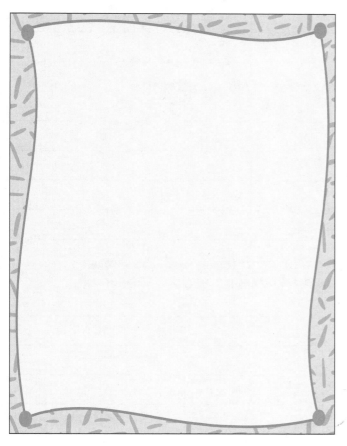

Details

1. _____

_____

2. _____

_____

3. _____

_____

4. _____

_____

5. _____

_____

What are Bud's thoughts about this picture? Find two quotes that show his thoughts. For each, use your own words to explain what the quote means.

Quote #1: _____

_____

What it means: _____

_____

Quote #2: _____

_____

What it means: _____

_____

NAME _____

THE PRETEND FAMILY

Answer the following questions about the events of Chapter 6.

1. Describe the attitude of the man at the back of the food line. How does he feel about Bud? What reason does this man give for feeling this way about Bud?

_____

_____

2. Who is Clarence? What is his first reaction to the square-faced man?

_____

3. How does Bud's pretend father act toward him? _____

_____

4. How does Bud's pretend mother act toward him? _____

_____

5. Compare and contrast the members of Bud's pretend family with the Amoses from earlier in the novel. Use evidence from the novel to support your answers.

This is how Mr. Amos acted: _____

_____

This is how Bud's pretend father is different: _____

_____

This is how Mrs. Amos acted: _____

_____

This is how Bud's pretend mother is different: _____

_____

This is how Todd Amos acted: _____

_____

This is how Bud's pretend brother is different: _____

_____

+ +

Considering Tone: The term **tone** refers to how the author feels about a character. How do you think the author feels about Bud's pretend family? Why do you think the author included them in the story? On the back of this paper, write a paragraph in which you answer these questions.

SIGNS OF THE TIMES

As Bud approaches the mission, he sees a large sign of a family. Once he goes inside the mission, there are more signs to read.

Sign Outside the Mission

Draw a picture of the sign here. Use the description from the novel to help you. If the sign has words on it, add those to your drawing.

How does Bud's pretend father react to this sign?

_____

_____

Why does he react this way?

_____

_____

_____

_____

_____

Signs Inside the Mission

Choose two of the signs inside the mission.

① What it says: _____

_____

Why it says this: _____

_____

② What it says: _____

_____

Why it says this: _____

_____

+ +

Considering Setting: The term **setting** refers not only to *where* a scene takes place but also *when* a scene takes place. How do these signs represent both the *where* and *when* of the setting? Why are they in this particular place? What do they say about this particular time in history? On the back of this paper, write a paragraph in which you explain your thoughts about these questions.

A SENSE OF PLACE

In Chapters 7 and 8, *Bud, Not Buddy* contains descriptive language that makes the settings come to life. Work with a partner to complete the chart below. Show how Christopher Paul Curtis' writing in these chapters appeals to our senses and allows us to better understand Bud's experiences.

	Chapter 7	Chapter 8
Where does this chapter mostly take place?		
Find words and phrases that describe images that appeal to the senses.	Sight:	Sight:
	Hearing	Hearing
	Touch:	Touch:
	Taste:	Taste:
	Smell:	Smell:

+ +

Considering Craft: Discuss the following questions with your partner. On the back of this paper, write a summary of your discussion.

✓ How are the chapters similar in how they use sensory words to show the setting?

✓ How are they different in how they do this?

✓ Which chapter best uses sensory images to make the reader feel the action and/or setting of the scene? Why?

NAME: _____

A NIGHT IN HOOVERVILLE

Answer the questions below about the events of Chapter 8.

1. In your own words, describe Hooverville. What do the homes look like, and who lives there?

   _____

   _____

   _____

2. Describe the three fires in Hooverville. What is the purpose of each?

   Fire #1: _____

   Fire #2: _____

   Fire #3: _____

3. Who is Hooverville named for? _____

   Why is it named for this person? _____

   _____

4. What happens to Bud during his night in Hooverville? Describe at least three events.

   _____

   _____

   _____

   _____

5. What happens in the morning after Bud's night in Hooverville? Describe at least three events that occur.

   _____

   _____

   _____

   _____

+ +

Considering Setting: Think about the author's description of Hooverville, the people who live there, and the events that happen. Describe how these elements give readers a sense of the time and place in which these people live. Use the back of this paper.

NAME _____

SECTION II LOG-IN

Now that you have finished this section of *Bud, Not Buddy*, take some time to add to your Interactive Novel Logs.

✦ **First, make a prediction about what will happen next in the novel.**

Use your "Crystal Ball" worksheet (page 19) to do this.

✦ **Next, make a more personal connection to what you have read.**

Choose one of the suggestions below and use it to fill a page in your Interactive Novel Log. Take this opportunity to connect with the novel in a way that appeals to you.

✦ ✦

Ideas for Your Interactive Novel Log

1
Old Photographs

In Chapter 5, Bud describes a photograph he has of his mother when she was a child. He wonders what was happening when the photo was taken and why she had the look on her face that she had. With permission, find a photograph of an older family member (parent, grandparent, etc.) when he/she was a child. Describe the photograph. Use the clues in the photograph to guess what was happening at that moment when it was taken.

2
Another Opens

In Chapter 5, Bud's mother tells him to remember that when one door closes, another opens. Can you think of an example of this from your life or from the life of someone you know? Write about this experience. Write about what happened and how you (or another person) felt when the first "door" closed and when the second one opened.

3
Sign of Success

In Chapter 6, the people in line for food must pass by a sign that says, "There's No Place Like America Today!" and shows a well-dressed family of four in a fancy car. This is known as a propaganda poster: it uses false or misleading images and words to make people have a certain feeling. This poster shows an idea of success that most people at that time could not realistically have. What picture would represent success in today's society? Create a propaganda poster for our times. Show what you think our society's idea of success is today.

4
Another Dream

In Chapter 8, Bud has a strange dream involving the man from the flyers and Deza Malone. Imagine another dream that Bud could have had. It can be as strange, silly, and weird as you want it to be, as long as it refers to characters, ideas, objects, or settings you have read about in these first eight chapters of the novel. You can use words to describe this dream, or you can draw some scenes from the dream—as if it were part of a comic book or graphic novel.

TEACHER INSTRUCTIONS

Section Note: Read Chapters 9–12 of the novel. In this section of the novel, Bud gets the idea that his next move must be to track down the man who he believes is his father.

After your students have read Chapters 9–12, have them begin their analyses of this section of the novel by completing the Interactive Novel Log activities on pages 11–18. Consult the "Teacher Instructions" on page 10 and distribute new copies of the following:

✦ **"The Summaries of Its Parts"** (page 11)
✦ **"Two Sides of Bud"** (page 12)
✦ **"Rules and Things"** (page 13)
✦ **"A Look Inside"** (page 14)

✦ **"Checking In on Theme"** (page 15)
✦ **"Making the Mood"** (page 16)
✦ **"Another Voice"** (page 17)
✦ **"Choice Words"** (page 18)

✦ ✦

Students will then further examine this section through the following worksheets:

Activity: "A Growing Idea" **Page #:** 36
Focus: Plot, Craft, Setting **Learning Type:** Individual
Description: Demonstrate an understanding of Bud's use of metaphor. (*TIP:* For the "Considering Setting" prompt, guide students to understand the clues given on the flyers. Consider allowing students access to atlases or the Internet.)

Activity: "The Road to Grand Rapids" **Page #:** 37
Focus: Setting, Plot **Learning Type:** Individual
Description: Examine the details of Bud's travels along the road at night. (*TIP:* For the "Research It" prompt, students will need brief Internet access.)

Activity: "They Have Their Reasons" **Page #:** 38
Focus: Plot, Characterization, Inference **Learning Type:** Individual
Description: Look closely at each character's motivations. Use inference.

Activity: "A Different Kind of Home" **Page #:** 39
Focus: Plot, Characterization **Learning Type:** Collaborative
Description: Work with a partner to discuss the relationships and dynamics between the characters in Lefty's family. Summarize discussions.

Activity: "On the Road" **Page #:** 40
Focus: Plot, Setting, Characterization **Learning Type:** Individual
Description: Examine the scene between Lefty and the policeman. Determine the reasons for each character's actions and/or thoughts.

Activity: "The Old Man" **Page #:** 41
Focus: Plot, Characterization **Learning Type:** Individual
Description: Use textual evidence to show Bud's feelings before and during his first meeting with Herman Calloway.

Activity: "Section III Log-In" **Page #:** 42
Focus: Plot, etc. **Learning Type:** Individual
Description: Complete "Crystal Ball" worksheets in order to predict future events in the novel. Then choose from several options to add to Interactive Novel Logs.

NAME: _____

A GROWING IDEA

In Chapter 9, Bud thinks back to when he first got the idea about Herman E. Calloway being his father. He uses a metaphor to describe how that idea grew bigger and bigger over time. A metaphor is a direct comparison between two things that are not at all alike in most ways but are alike in one specific way.

1. What metaphor does Bud use to describe his idea that Herman E. Calloway is his father? To what does he compare this idea?

   _____

   Find a quote that shows this: _____

   _____ Page number(s): _____

2. Bud thinks about the different stages that led to this idea growing from something small to something very large. Choose three of those steps or stages that happened during that process.

What happened **first**?	What happened **next**?	What happened **after that**?
_____ _____ _____	_____ _____ _____	_____ _____ _____
How did this "grow" the idea? _____ _____ _____	How did this "grow" the idea? _____ _____ _____	How did this "grow" the idea? _____ _____ _____

+ +

Considering Setting: Just before Bud heads west to Grand Rapids, he takes one last look at the flyers he carries around in his suitcase. The last two flyers don't include pictures of the band; instead, there are just drawings. Why do you think this is? Use the clues given on the flyers to help you answer this question. Think about the time period in which the story takes place. Also think about the band names and places written on the two flyers without pictures. (**Hint:** If needed, look up the cities mentioned on the last two flyers to see where they are located.) Write your ideas on the back of this paper.

NAME: _____

THE ROAD TO GRAND RAPIDS

In Chapter 9, Bud researches his trip to Grand Rapids. In Chapter 10, he starts out for the city where he believes his father lives.

1. How long does Bud think it will take him to walk to Grand Rapids? Show the math Bud uses to determine this information.

2. Bud's journey begins in Flint. Before he begins, he writes down the names of some cities he will need to pass through on his way to Grand Rapids. Write four of these city names on the diagram below.

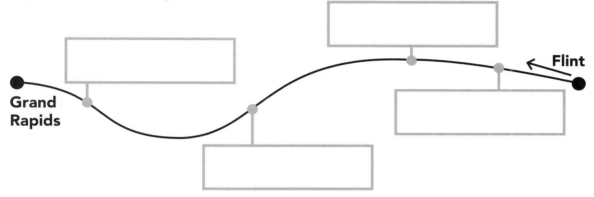

3. On his trip, Bud notices a big difference between the country and the city. He even sees signs that announce which part he is entering or leaving. Complete the chart.

	Describe the road Bud sees.	What does the sign on this side say?	Describe the sounds Bud hears.
City			
Country			

4. A man stops his car to find Bud. At what time and in what city does this happen?

_____

+ +

Research It: Use online tools or another source to determine how far Bud walked along the road to Grand Rapids. In an online search engine, you can type in "Distance between Flint, Michigan and [the name of the city where the man pulls over and picks up Bud]." Complete the sentences below.

a. In total, Bud walked about _____ miles before he was picked up by the man.

b. If that is true, then this means that Bud had been walking for about _____ hours.

NAME: _____

THEY HAVE THEIR REASONS

1. What is the man's main reason for wanting to pick Bud up?

_____

_____

Find a quote that gives you this information: _____

_____ Page number(s): _____

2. What is Bud's main reason for getting in the man's car?

_____

_____

Find a quote that gives you this information: _____

_____ Page number(s): _____

3. How does the man seem to feel about being in this place at this time?

_____

Find a quote that gives you this information: _____

_____ Page number(s): _____

4. What is the main reason why Bud tries to drive away from the man? Why is Bud afraid of the man?

_____

_____

5. Several times, the man says he will never forget the sight of Bud driving off in his car? Name the two main reasons why this sight caused great fear for him. (**Hint:** Think about where this takes place and why the man is there at this time of night.)

_____

_____

_____

How did you know this information? Does the author tell you this? Or do you have to infer it? To *infer* is to use the clues given to arrive at a logical conclusion. Explain.

_____

_____

_____

NAME(S): _____

A DIFFERENT KIND OF HOME

Chapter 11 ends with Buddy waking up and eating breakfast in the Sleets' house. Work with a partner to answer the following questions.

1. What does Buddy learn while he is pretending to be asleep? Name three things.

_____

_____

_____

2. Other than Buddy, who are the four people in the house that morning? Complete the chart. Write in each person's name and his/her relationship to the other people.

Character's Name	Relationship to Each of the Other Characters

3. Think about the breakfast scene. With your partner, talk about the following:

- how the family acts around one another
- how they act while they eat
- what they eat
- how Bud feels about these things

Summarize your discussion here.

_____

_____

_____

_____

4. Think back to Chapter 6. (Reread that chapter, if needed.) How are Lefty and the Sleet family similar to Bud's pretend family at the mission? How are they different? Discuss with your partner. Summarize your discussion here.

_____

_____

_____

_____

NAME: _____

ON THE ROAD

After breakfast at Mrs. Sleet's house, Bud and Lefty take off for Grand Rapids.

1. On the way to Grand Rapids, Lefty's car is pulled over by a policeman. Why?

   _____

   _____

2. Look back at this incident with the policeman. What is really happening? Name three things done by Lefty and/or the policeman. For each one, show how Bud gets the wrong idea. Tell what he thinks is happening.

   a.

What Is Really Happening	What Bud Thinks Is Happening

   b. What do you think the policeman's actions tell us about this time in U.S. history?

   _____

   _____

   c. What do you think Lefty's words, actions, and reasons for doing things during this scene tell us about him?

   _____

   _____

3. Earlier on the ride, Lefty tells Bud about the telegram he has sent to Calloway. Lefty explains how telegrams work. In your own words, paraphrase this information.

   _____

   _____

   _____

+ +

Try It Out: Use Lefty's explanation of how telegrams work to write a telegram. On the back of this paper, write one from Bud to Deza Malone. Explain where he's going, why he's going there, or whatever other information you think he'd want to share with Deza. Remember, though, that more letters mean more money, so keep it short.

NAME: _____

THE OLD MAN

In Chapter 12, Bud finally meets the man he thinks is his father.

1. How does Bud feel as he and Lefty approach the Log Cabin?

_____

_____

Find a quote that shows this: _____

_____ Page number(s): _____

2. How does Bud convince Lefty to allow him to go into the Log Cabin alone? On what condition does Lefty agree to let Bud do this?

_____

_____

_____

3. Once inside the Log Cabin, Bud first lays eyes on Herman Calloway.

   a. What about Herman convinces Bud that he is his father?

   _____

   _____

   _____

   Find a quote that shows this: _____

   _____ Page number(s): _____

   b. What about Herman makes Bud doubt that he is his father?

   _____

   _____

   _____

   Find a quote that shows this: _____

   _____ Page number(s): _____

+ +

Picture It: Imagine if *Bud, Not Buddy* were a comic book or graphic novel. On the back of this paper, draw a picture of the final moment of Chapter 12. You may include some words in and around your picture, but the story of the moment should mostly come from the visual details you add to your picture.

NAME: _____

SECTION III LOG-IN

Now that you have finished this section of *Bud, Not Buddy*, take some time to add to your Interactive Novel Logs.

✦ **First, make a prediction about what will happen next in the novel.**

Use your "Crystal Ball" worksheet (page 19) to do this.

✦ **Next, make a more personal connection to what you have read.**

Choose one of the suggestions below and use it to fill a page in your Interactive Novel Log. Take this opportunity to connect with the novel in a way that appeals to you.

✦ ✦

Ideas for Your Interactive Novel Log

1
A Mighty Maple

Bud says that his idea that Herman E. Calloway is his father started as a little seed and grew into a mighty maple tree. Have you had a similar experience? Do you remember how something started as a little idea and grew to something that was very important to you? Write about that experience. Or instead, you could use pictures or diagrams to show how your idea grew.

2
A Long, Dark Journey

In this section, Bud decides to walk from Flint to Grand Rapids. He does this all alone and at night. Imagine such a journey. What would it be like for you? Divide your page into thirds. Explain your thoughts **before** undertaking such a journey, **during** the journey, and **after** you have completed your travels. At each stage, you could choose to compare your situation to Bud's.

3
Unlike Any Other

In Chapter 11, Bud has breakfast with Lefty's family. The way the family acts during the meal is unlike anything Bud has ever experienced. Have you ever been a guest at another family's house and observed that they do things differently than you're used to? Write about the experience. What was so different? Do you think you could get used to this difference, or do you like to stick with what is familiar to you?

4
A Natural

As soon as Bud hears Herman talking, he is convinced that he is hearing his father. The natural way that Herman tells a story reminds Bud of himself. Who is the best storyteller you know? Describe this person and explain what makes him or her such a great spinner of tales.

Let me tell you a story about the best storyteller I know . . .

TEACHER INSTRUCTIONS

Section Note: Read Chapters 13–15 of the novel. In this section of *Bud, Not Buddy*, we are introduced to the members of the band, and we see the different ways they respond to Bud's insistence that he is Herman's son. A night of good food and good times causes an emotional reaction in Bud.

After your students have read Chapters 13–15, have them begin their analyses of this section of the novel by completing the Interactive Novel Log activities on pages 11–18. Consult the "Teacher Instructions" on page 10 and distribute new copies of the following:

- ✦ **"The Summaries of Its Parts"** (page 11)
- ✦ **"Two Sides of Bud"** (page 12)
- ✦ **"Rules and Things"** (page 13)
- ✦ **"A Look Inside"** (page 14)

- ✦ **"Checking In on Theme"** (page 15)
- ✦ **"Making the Mood"** (page 16)
- ✦ **"Another Voice"** (page 17)
- ✦ **"Choice Words"** (page 18)

+ +

Students will then further examine this section through the following worksheets:

Activity: "Player Cards"
Focus: Characterization
Page #: 44
Learning Type: Individual/Collaborative
Description: Create player cards for each member of Herman Calloway's band. List names, nicknames, and roles in the band. Then, work in groups to describe each band member's personality. Find and cite evidence to support claims.

Activity: "Say What They Mean"
Focus: Characterization, Plot, Voice
Page #: 45
Learning Type: Collaborative
Description: Work with a partner to locate idiomatic quotes from the novel and to provide the following information about each quote: who said it, what was meant by it, and how you and your partner used clues in the novel to determine the quote's meaning.

Activity: "Home Cooking"
Focus: Plot, Characterization, Craft
Page #: 46
Learning Type: Individual
Description: Use a passage in the novel as inspiration to list the "ingredients" that combined to make Bud cry at the Sweet Pea restaurant. Use evidence from the novel to explain Bud's reaction to this combination of ingredients.

Activity: "A Night at the Station"
Focus: Plot, Inference
Page #: 47
Learning Type: Individual
Description: Examine Bud's night in Herman Calloway's home. Use inference to determine and understand the events of the plot.

Activity: "Section IV Log-In"
Focus: Plot, etc.
Page #: 48
Learning Type: Individual
Description: Complete "Crystal Ball" worksheets in order to predict future events in the novel. Then choose from several options to add to Interactive Novel Logs.

NAME: _____

PLAYER CARDS

In this section, Bud meets the members of the band. There are seven in all. Write each one's name, nickname (if any), and instrument/role in the band. In the box at the top left, write the band's current name and the place where they are currently playing.

	Name?	Name?	Name?
	Nickname?	Nickname?	Nickname?
	Instrument/Role?	Instrument/Role?	Instrument/Role?
Name?	Name?	Name?	Name?
Nickname?	Nickname?	Nickname?	Nickname?
Instrument/Role?	Instrument/Role?	Instrument/Role?	Instrument/Role?

+ +

Considering Characterization: Work in groups. Together, decide how your group would describe each band member's personality. Together, find an example that shows this personality. On a separate piece of paper, write statements about each band member. Follow this format:

> [Band member's name] is [personality trait]. For example, [evidence from the novel showing this person to have this trait].

NAME(S): _____

SAY WHAT THEY MEAN

The members of Herman's band have a way of speaking that is not always familiar to Bud. Their speech is filled with idioms, metaphors, and other colorful phrases.

Each of the phrases below can be found in Chapter 13. Work with a partner to find each one. Record who says it, and explain what that person means by it.

Phrase #1

". . . be careful, that's my bread and butter in there."

Who says it? _____ What does he mean by it?_____

_____

How did you and your partner determine this?

_____

_____

Phrase #2

". . . this is your little red wagon, you pull it if you want."

Who says it? _____ What does he mean by it?_____

_____

How did you and your partner determine this?

_____

_____

Phrase #3

". . . you're going to have to lay off the kid's chops"

Who says it? _____ What does he mean by it?_____

_____

How did you and your partner determine this?

_____

_____

Phrase #4

"What you see in that front seat is a man on borrowed time."

Who says it? _____ What does he mean by it?_____

_____

How did you and your partner determine this?

_____

_____

NAME: _____

HOME COOKING

In Chapter 14, Bud gets to eat at a restaurant for the first time. As he walks in to the Sweet Pea, he is struck by a dizzying array of smells. All of these scents combine to form the greatest smell he has ever experienced. Later, another combination of things leads to a new experience for Bud. Sitting in the restaurant, Bud begins to cry, and he can't stop. What led to that moment?

In the pot below, list the ingredients that combined to make Bud cry. Each ingredient should name a thing and also the person(s) who provided it. A first one is written in for you.

a heaping helping of ___*good food from the Sweet Pea*___

a taste of _____

a touch of _____

a dash of _____

a hint of _____

a whole lot of _____

How and why do these ingredients combine to make Bud cry? Explain. In your answer, use a quote from the novel to support your claim.

_____

_____

_____

_____

_____

_____

_____

A NIGHT AT THE STATION

After leaving the Sweet Pea, Bud is taken back to Herman Calloway's home. Answer the following questions about the events of Chapter 15.

1. What is the nickname of Herman's house? _____

2. Why is it nicknamed that? Explain where the nickname comes from.

_____

_____

3. Describe the room in which Bud is allowed to sleep.

_____

_____

_____

4. Why does Bud think that the room belongs to a dead girl?

_____

_____

5. Miss Thomas lets Bud know the layout of the house. Label the doors below to show where everyone is sleeping in the house and where the bathroom is located. Bud's room is labeled for you.

Bud's room		

hallway

6. After Miss Thomas leaves the room the first time, she has a loud argument with Herman. What do she and Herman argue about?

_____

_____

How do you know this? How can you infer this information from what Herman does next?

_____

_____

NAME: _____

SECTION IV LOG-IN

Now that you have finished this section of *Bud, Not Buddy*, take some time to add to your Interactive Novel Logs.

✦ **First, make a prediction about what will happen next in the novel.**
 Use your "Crystal Ball" worksheet (page 19) to do this.

✦ **Next, make a more personal connection to what you have read.**
 Choose one of the suggestions below and use it to fill a page in your Interactive Novel Log. Take this opportunity to connect with the novel in a way that appeals to you.

✦ ✦

Ideas for Your Interactive Novel Log

1
Part of a Band

In Chapter 13, Bud observes Herman's band talking to each other and interacting with one another. They have a way of speaking that shows how familiar they are with each other. They understand one another. Think about how you and your friends talk and interact. Write about the way you and your friends speak to one another. Explain the things you each understand that other people might not understand as easily. Or write a short dialogue showing that speech.

2
Best Restaurant Ever

In Chapter 14, Bud eats at his first restaurant, the Sweet Pea, and he is convinced that it must be the best restaurant in the world. Convince Bud that he is wrong. Write him a note. Explain your choice for the best restaurant you've been to. Give reasons why it is even better than the Sweet Pea.

3
Making Scents

When Bud walks into the Sweet Pea, he smells (and describes the smell of) a whole slew of scents. It is said that our sense of smell is the one that is most closely linked to memory. Can you remember a time when you smelled a combination of powerfully good (or powerfully bad) smells? Describe those smells. Pattern your description after Bud's description of the smells inside the Sweet Pea.

4
Ghosts and Monsters

When Bud spends the night in Grand Calloway Station, he worries about ghosts and monsters entering the room through the closet doors and in various other ways. Write your feelings about Bud's worries. Do you understand his fears? Did you fear certain places in your room or in other people's houses? Do you have a younger sibling who has similar fears? Write about your experiences with these fears that are very common to children at night.

TEACHER INSTRUCTIONS

Section Note: Read Chapters 16–19 of the novel. In this final section of *Bud, Not Buddy*, Bud learns the truth about his connection to Herman Calloway.

After your students have read Chapters 16–19, have them begin their analyses of this section of the novel by completing the Interactive Novel Log activities on pages 11–18. Consult the "Teacher Instructions" on page 10 and distribute new copies of the following:

- ✦ **"The Summaries of Its Parts"** (page 11)
- ✦ **"Two Sides of Bud"** (page 12)
- ✦ **"Rules and Things"** (page 13)
- ✦ **"A Look Inside"** (page 14)

- ✦ **"Checking In on Theme"** (page 15)
- ✦ **"Making the Mood"** (page 16)
- ✦ **"Another Voice"** (page 17)
- ✦ **"Choice Words"** (page 18)

✦ ✦

Students will then further examine this section through the following worksheets:

Activity: "The Decision"　　　　　　　　　　**Page #:** 50
Focus: Plot, Characterization　　　　　　　　**Learning Type:** Individual
Description: Examine the morning after Bud's first night at Grand Calloway Station. Determine the decision that is made about his future, the conditions he will be expected to meet, and the various reactions of the other characters. Take a closer look at the gifts Bud receives.

Activity: "Part of the Band"　　　　　　　　　**Page #:** 51
Focus: Plot, Characterization, Theme　　　　　**Learning Type:** Individual
Description: Consider how the band shows its acceptance of Bud. Detail the process the band uses to determine Bud's band nickname.

Activity: "Capturing Sound"　　　　　　　　　**Page #:** 52
Focus: Craft, Imagery　　　　　　　　　　　　**Learning Type:** Individual
Description: Analyze the way imagery is used to describe the various sounds Bud hears when the band plays. Cite evidence to illustrate the author's use of descriptive language.

Activity: "What We Learn"　　　　　　　　　　**Page #:** 53
Focus: Plot, Setting, Inference　　　　　　　　**Learning Type:** Individual
Description: Examine the things Bud discovers in Chapter 18. First, look at Dirty Deed's role in the band and why it is necessary in the time and place in which the novel is set. Then use clues to infer the sequence of past events.

Activity: "In the End"　　　　　　　　　　　　**Page #:** 54
Focus: Craft, Plot, Point of View　　　　　　　**Learning Type:** Collaborative
Description: Work with a partner to discuss the way the novel ends and the effect the final events have on the various characters.

Activity: "Section V Log-In"　　　　　　　　　**Page #:** 55
Focus: Plot, etc.　　　　　　　　　　　　　　**Learning Type:** Individual
Description: Use "Crystal Ball" worksheets to predict future events in the lives of the characters. Then choose from several options to add to Interactive Novel Logs.

NAME: _____

THE DECISION

In Chapter 16, Bud wakes up to a new life.

1. What decision was made while Bud slept?

_____

_____

2. What are some of the characters' reactions to this news? Provide a quote from Chapter 16 to show each person's reaction.

Character	Reaction	Quote that Shows Reaction
Bud		
Miss Thomas		
Herman		
Dirty Deed		

3. How will Bud be expected to "pull [his] own weight"?

_____

_____

4. Name the two gifts Bud is given by Eddie. Explain the purpose of each.

 What is it? _____

Why is he given it? _____

_____

_____

 What is it? _____

Why is he given it? _____

_____

_____

PART OF THE BAND

Later in Chapter 16, the band decides that if Bud is to be part of their band, he must get something first.

1. What do the men in the band decide that Bud needs in order to be a member? How does this decision show their acceptance of Bud as one of them?

_____

_____

2. How does Miss Thomas feel about this idea? Answer in your own words.

_____

_____

Now find a quote that shows her thoughts about it: _____

_____

_____ Found on page number(s): _____

3. On what nickname does the band decide? Write it on the sign below.

Introducing

4. How do they arrive at this nickname? Use your own words to explain the process.

_____

_____

_____

_____

5. How does Bud feel about his new nickname? Use your own words to answer.

_____

Now find a quote that shows his thoughts about it: _____

_____

_____ Found on page number(s): _____

NAME: _____

CAPTURING SOUND

For most of Chapter 17, Bud listens to the band warm up and play a song. Notice how the author of *Bud, Not Buddy* describes the music Bud hears. The sounds of the instruments are often compared to other sounds from the world around us. Choose three descriptions. Tell who is playing the sound, provide a quote that shows how the author describes the sound, and explain what sound in nature the author is comparing the music to.

**Sound
#1**

Player of the sound: _____

Quote that shows how the author describes the sound:

_____

_____

Comparison author makes: _____

_____

**Sound
#2**

Player of the sound: _____

Quote that shows how the author describes the sound:

_____

_____

Comparison author makes: _____

_____

**Sound
#3**

Player of the sound: _____

Quote that shows how the author describes the sound:

_____

_____

Comparison author makes: _____

_____

✦ ✦

Considering Craft: What does the author do to make the music come alive for the reader? In your opinion, how well does he accomplish this? As you read, can you "hear" the music the band is playing? On the back of this paper, explain your thoughts.

NAME: _____

WHAT WE LEARN

In Chapter 18, the readers learn a few things both big and small about the characters.

1. Why does Thug say that Dirty Deed is in the band? Answer in one sentence.

_____

_____

2. Why is it important for Herman to have someone like Dirty Deed in his band? Give two reasons that have to do with the setting in which the novel takes place.

_____

_____

_____

_____

3. How do Herman and Bud end up traveling in a car without the rest of the band?

_____

_____

4. What does Herman do just before he gets into the car to drive home?

_____

_____

5. What does Bud find in the glove box of Herman's car? Give details.

_____

_____

6. From the information we are given, we can infer a sequence of events that led to Bud having these objects in his suitcase. Show each step. One is done for you.

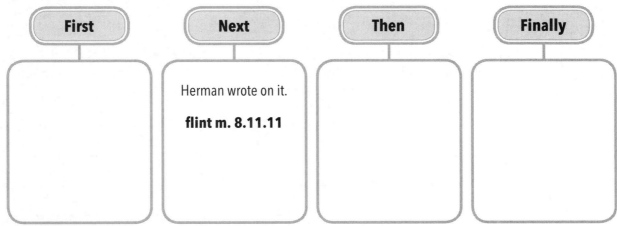

First	Next	Then	Finally
	Herman wrote on it. **flint m. 8.11.11**		

NAME(S): _____

IN THE END

Work with a partner to discuss the ideas presented in the final chapter of *Bud, Not Buddy*.

Discuss the passage in which Miss Thomas explains to Bud how Herman is taking the news of what he has just learned. What idea is she trying to get Bud to understand? Together, put this idea into your own words and record them below.

_____

_____

_____

At the end, why does Bud give the flyers and most of his rocks to Herman? Why do you think he keeps the one with "flint" written on it? Discuss this with your partner. On the lines below, summarize your discussion.

_____

_____

_____

In what way(s) is the ending of *Bud, Not Buddy* a happy one for its characters? Discuss this with your partner. On the lines below, summarize your discussion. Underline or circle your best point.

_____

_____

_____

_____

In what way(s) is the ending of *Bud, Not Buddy* a sad one for its characters? Discuss this with your partner. Summarize your discussion. Then underline or circle your best point for why the ending is a sad one.

_____

_____

_____

_____

NAME: _____

SECTION V LOG-IN

Now that you have finished this section of *Bud, Not Buddy*, take some time to add to your Interactive Novel Logs.

✦ **First, make a prediction about what will happen next in the characters' lives.**

Use your "Crystal Ball" worksheet (page 19) to do this.

✦ **On a separate piece of paper, write a proposal for a sequel to the novel.**

How would you write the next several chapters in the story of Bud? Which characters, settings, and events would you include? How would your sequel honor the original novel, while also being an exciting addition to it?

✦ **Finally, make a more personal connection to what you have read.**

Choose one of the suggestions below and use it to fill a page in your Interactive Novel Log. Take this opportunity to connect with the novel in a way that appeals to you.

✦ ✦

Ideas for Your Interactive Novel Log

1
Musical Musings

In Chapter 17, there is a lengthy description of the various sounds the band combines to form their music. Think about a song you love. Describe the various parts of that song in a way that is a similar to how the author of *Bud, Not Buddy* describes the music of Herman's band. How would you describe each element of your song and the way these elements come together to form its overall sound?

2
Words of Advice

At the end of the book, the mystery has been solved, and Bud and Herman now know how they are connected. Now that Bud knows that Herman is his grandfather, what do you think he should say when he discovers Herman crying in the girl's room? Do you think Bud handles the situation in the best way? What words of advice would you give to Bud if you could?

3
Band Flyer

Imagine a future where Bud has become a great saxophonist. Create a band flyer that shows the band and introduces Bud as their newest member. Remember to add details like the band's name, the date of the show, and where the band is playing. Be as creative as you like, but try to make the poster realistic for the time and place of the novel.

4
Familiar and New

Did any of the events from the novel remind you of the events from a different novel or film? Were there any events or descriptions that were completely unlike any you have ever read or seen in any other novel or film? Create a chart that shows what was familiar about the book and/or what was new to you.

TEACHER INSTRUCTIONS

After your students have finished reading *Bud, Not Buddy*, they can further their in-depth analyses of the novel through the use of the following worksheets:

+ +

Activity: "Add It Up"   **Page #:** 57–59   **Learning Type:** Individual
Description: Use the work done in the Interactive Novel Logs to sum up thoughts on the novel as a whole.

Activity: "An Important Scene"   **Page #:** 60   **Learning Type:** Individual
Description: Highlight a scene, consider a different ending, and state how this would alter the novel's plot.

Activity: "The WOW Factor"   **Page #:** 61   **Learning Type:** Individual
Description: Examine a particularly memorable scene from the novel. Record the 5 Ws about the scene.

Activity: "A New Point of View"   **Page #:** 62   **Learning Type:** Individual
Description: Analyze the author's use of the first-person perspective and determine how the novel would be altered if it were written in third-person. Rewrite a scene in third-person.

Activity: "Acting Out"   **Page #:** 63   **Learning Type:** Collaborative
Description: In groups, think about conversations that must have taken place when Bud was not around to witness them. Write a script and perform it in front of the class. (**TIP:** Divide the class into groups of 3–5 members.)

Activity: "Historical Fiction"   **Page #:** 64   **Learning Type:** Individual
Description: Look at the elements of historical fiction and show how this novel approaches those elements.

Activity: "Historical Figures"   **Page #:** 65   **Learning Type:** Individual
Description: Research the historical figures mentioned in the novel. Decide what these figures tell us about Bud.

Activity: "Considering Genre"   **Page #:** 66   **Learning Type:** Individual
Description: Examine Bud's fears and how they belong to a different genre. Rewrite a scene in this genre. (**Note:** Although this activity is consistent with the themes and voice of the novel, it may not be appropriate for all classrooms.)

Activity: "Considering Voice"   **Page #:** 67   **Learning Type:** Individual
Description: Define Bud's voice. Consider how the novel would be different if Bud had a much different voice.

Activity: "An Elemental Choice"   **Page #:** 68–69   **Learning Type:** Individual
Description: Plan and write a persuasive essay on which element most makes the novel special: voice, plot, setting, or theme. Complete the outline form and use a self-editing checklist to hone the essay prior to writing a final draft.

Activity: "A Novel Poster"   **Page #:** 70–71   **Learning Type:** Collaborative
Description: Create a poster that identifies the elements that contribute to a chapter's success.

Activity: "A Persuasive Letter"   **Page #:** 72   **Learning Type:** Individual
Description: Use a letter-writing format to construct an argument and support that opinion with evidence from the text.

Activity: "My Book Rating"   **Page #:** 73   **Learning Type:** Individual
Description: Use a rating system to evaluate different components of the story before making a final evaluation of the book as a whole.

NAME: _____

ADD IT UP

A novel is the sum of its parts. It is a combination of the events (plot) and people (characters) it describes. Look back at the work you have done as you have read each section of *Bud, Not Buddy*. Decide how the parts add up to form the novel as a whole.

The Summaries of Its Parts

Now that you have finished the novel — and have had a lot of practice with summarization — use your skills to write a very brief summary of the entire novel. Fit your statement on the lines below. In order to do so, you must choose to include only the most important events.

_____

_____

_____

_____

_____

_____

_____

_____

Now your teacher will read you the Book Summary included in the teacher guide (page 7). Listen closely and answer the following questions.

1. Was there anything you felt this summary should have included but did not?

_____

_____

_____

2. Would this summary give someone who hasn't read the book a good idea of what to expect? Explain your answer.

_____

_____

_____

3. Would you say that *Bud, Not Buddy* is easy or difficult to summarize? Explain.

_____

_____

_____

NAME: _____

ADD IT UP (CONT.)

Two Sides of Bud

Now that you have finished the novel, which would you say is the side that most defines Bud: his wise, street-smart side or his young, immature side? Check the box beside your answer. On the lines below, use evidence from the novel to defend your choice.

❑ Bud is street-smart and wise beyond his years.

❑ Bud is immature and thinks/acts like a child.

_____

_____

_____

_____

_____

_____

Rules and Things

Look back at some of Bud's Rules and Things to Have a Funner Life and Make a Better Liar Out of Yourself. Choose one that you feel was a wise rule for Bud to make for himself. Choose one that you feel was not so wise. Use examples to defend your choices.

One Wise Rule: _____

_____

When he mentions this rule: _____

_____

Why it's wise: _____

_____

One Not-So-Wise Rule: _____

_____

When he mentions this rule: _____

_____

Why it's not so wise: _____

_____

ADD IT UP (CONT.)

Checking In on Theme

Of all the themes introduced in *Bud, Not Buddy*, which do you feel is the most important theme? Check off one box, and then explain your choice on the lines below.

❑ compassion   ❑ home   ❑ poverty

❑ family   ❑ lies   ❑ race

❑ fear   ❑ perseverance   ❑ wisdom

_____

_____

_____

_____

_____

_____

_____

_____

_____

Crystal Ball

Look back at your predictions for each section of *Bud, Not Buddy*.

1. Which of your predictions came true just like you thought they would?

_____

_____

2. Which of your predictions were very different from what ended up happening? Choose one, and explain the different direction the story might have gone if your prediction had come true.

_____

_____

_____

_____

NAME: _____

AN IMPORTANT SCENE

Choose one important scene in the novel to analyze. Complete each form below

Tell It Like It Is

Page numbers of the scene: _____ What happens in the scene? _____

_____

_____

_____

How does this scene fit into the whole novel?

_____

_____

_____

Tell It Like It Could Have Been

Think of another way the scene could have ended. Describe the new ending here.

_____

_____

_____

_____

If the scene had ended that way, how would the rest of the story change?

The new ending would have caused this to happen: _____

_____

Here is why: _____

_____

_____

Would this change have made the story better or worse? Explain.

_____

_____

_____

NAME: _____

THE WOW FACTOR

The novel *Bud, Not Buddy* is filled with scenes that are exciting, funny, sad, joyful, and/or touching. Which scene most wowed you? Choose that scene and list the 5 Ws (*who, what, where, when,* and *why*).

Who
was in the scene?

What
happens in the scene?

When
in the novel does this happen?

Where
does the scene take place?

Why
is this scene so memorable?

Now answer one final question: **How** *does this scene change or affect the plot of the rest of the novel?*

_____

_____

NAME: _____

A NEW POINT OF VIEW

Bud, Not Buddy is written in first-person point of view. This means that the author uses pronouns such as "I" and "me" when writing about Bud's experiences. It also means that we the readers can only experience what Bud experiences. We can't know what other people are thinking or what they're doing when Bud is not around. When a novel is written in third-person point of view, the author uses pronouns such as "he" and "him." In third-person narration, we can know what each character is thinking.

Choose an important scene from the novel. Rewrite a few paragraphs from that scene. This time, however, use the third-person point of view to show what happens during the scene.

The scene I chose is _____

If the novel had been written in third-person, this scene would read more like this:

_____

_____

_____

_____

_____

_____

_____

_____

_____

_____

_____

1. How do you think the novel would have changed if the author had used the third-person point of view?

_____

_____

_____

2. Why do you think the author chose to use first-person perspective in this novel?

_____

_____

ACTING OUT

Since *Bud, Not Buddy* is told from Bud's perspective, we are only able to witness what Bud witnesses. But we know that in the world of the novel, the other characters' lives go on even when Bud is not around to see and hear them.

With your group, create a scene that must have taken place in the novel. Choose from these options:

Scene #1

What happens: The Amos family wakes up in the morning after Bud escapes the shed.

Characters: Mr. Amos, Mrs. Amos, Todd Amos

Scene #2

What happens: Bud's pretend family talk about their breakfast with Bud at the mission.

Characters: the mother, father, brother, and sister

Scene #3

What happens: The people in Hooverville discuss what happens after the police leave.

Characters: Deza Malone, the mouth organ man, others

Scene #4

What happens: Lefty explains to his family why he is bringing Bud to stay with them for the night.

Characters: Lefty Lewis, the Sleet family

Scene #5

What happens: During Bud's first night at Herman's house, the band discusses what to do with him.

Characters: Miss Thomas, Herman, Eddie, other band members

As a group, choose your scene. Brainstorm ideas about the conversation that must have taken place in your scene. Work together to write a script or come up with ideas. (Use the tips provided below.) Perform the scene in front of your class.

Tips for Writing Dialogue

✦ Write the speaking character's name, followed by a colon. After the colon, write the words said by the character.

   Example: Herman: I don't want anything to do with that boy!

✦ Each character's voice should be consistent with how that person speaks or thinks in the novel.

NAME: _____

HISTORICAL FICTION

Bud, Not Buddy is written in the genre of historical fiction. The diagram below shows the qualities a novel must have to fit into this genre.

Historical Fiction

Setting	**Plot**	**Characters**
The novel must be set in a specific time in the past. It may also be set in a specific place where historical events occurred.	The events that happen to the main character(s) are imagined by the author, but real events from history can occur, too.	Most characters are created by the author, although real historical figures may be mentioned or may play a role in the plot.

+ +

Think about how *Bud, Not Buddy* fits into the genre of historical fiction. For each element listed above, write your thoughts about the novel.

1. Why is the period of time in which the novel is set an important element of the novel?

   _____

   _____

2. Why is the place in which the novel is set an important element of the novel?

   _____

   _____

3. How is the plot influenced by real events that took place during this time in history? Give at least two examples.

   _____

   _____

4. Are the characters mostly taken from history or created by the author?

   _____

   _____

5. What about this period of time in history inspired the author to create these characters?

   _____

   _____

NAME: _____

HISTORICAL FIGURES

Many historical figures are mentioned in *Bud, Not Buddy*. The list below shows several of these. (The chapter in which the name is mentioned is listed in parentheses.)

Do research to find out a little bit about each one. In the right column, write a brief phrase describing each and his/her importance in history. In the left column, name the character who said this name (or thought it) in the novel.

Character	Historical Figure	Brief Description
	John Dillinger (2)	
	J. Edgar Hoover (4)	
	Pretty Boy Floyd (5)	
	President Herbert Hoover (8)	
	Baby Face Nelson (10)	
	Ruth Dandridge (11)	
	George Washington Carver (11)	
	Machine Gun Kelly (12)	
	John Brown, abolitionist (12)	
	Blind Lemon Jefferson (14)	

+ +

Considering Characterization: Look back at the people that Bud mentions or thinks about. Do they seem to have anything in common? If so, what do you think this says about Bud as a character? Why does he tend to think about these types of people?

_____

_____

_____

_____

©Teacher Created Resources   65   *#2977 In-Depth Guide for Bud, Not Buddy*

NAME: _____

CONSIDERING GENRE

We know that *Bud, Not Buddy* is a work of historical fiction, but sometimes it seems that Bud thinks he may be in a completely different novel that was written in a completely different genre. Sometimes, he seems to think he may be in a horror novel. The horror genre involves evil monsters, gory deaths, and dangers that lurk behind every corner.

+ +

First: Think back to Bud's thoughts, worries, and concerns. List the ones that seem to come from the horror genre.

_____

_____

_____

Next: Choose a scene from *Bud, Not Buddy*. Imagine how this scene would be different if this book had been written in the horror genre (and if all of Bud's deepest fears were true). Rewrite the scene in this genre. (**Note:** Something that is written in the horror genre can still be silly or funny if you want it to be!)

_____

_____

_____

_____

_____

_____

_____

_____

_____

_____

_____

_____

_____

_____

_____

_____

CONSIDERING VOICE

Every literary character has a voice. In literature, the term **voice** does not usually refer to the sound a character's vocal cords make when he/she speaks. It refers to the style and characteristics of that character's speech. In other words, it's about the words the character uses and the way he/she uses them. With that in mind, how would you describe Bud's voice?

	Check the box beside the __best__ answer.	Find a quote that shows this.
a. Bud	❑ is very calm. ❑ is very excitable.	
b. Bud	❑ does not exaggerate. ❑ exaggerates a lot.	
c. Bud	❑ doesn't think too much about things. ❑ analyzes people.	

1. Collect your thoughts about Bud's voice here. Do your best to write one sentence that sums up his voice.

   _____

   _____

2. Why do you think the author chose this voice for Bud? How is the novel well-served by having a narrator with this type of voice?

   _____

   _____

3. Now think of a very different voice than Bud's. What would such a voice be like? On the lines below, describe a voice that is very different from Bud's.

   _____

   _____

4. Can you imagine what the novel would be like if Bud had the voice you just described? How would this change the novel? Would the change be for the good of the novel? Or would the novel suffer because of this new voice? Explain your thoughts.

   _____

   _____

+ +

Give It a Try: On the back of this paper, rewrite a scene from the novel. Use this new voice that you have just described.

NAME: _____

AN ELEMENTAL CHOICE

Four terms we might use to discuss a work of literature are *voice*, *plot*, *setting*, and *theme*.

Voice	Plot	Setting	Theme
the speech and thought patterns of the narrator	the events that take place in the novel	the place and time in which a story is set	the underlying idea(s) or message(s) in the novel

Write an essay in which you argue that one of these elements is the most important part of *Bud, Not Buddy*. Follow the outline below and on the following page. Use the space provided to brainstorm ideas and to plan your rough draft.

Paragraph 1 — Set up your essay by introducing the four terms and giving a brief description of how each element is used in the novel.

How **Voice** is used: _____

_____

Why it's important: _____

_____

How **Plot** is used: _____

_____

Why it's important: _____

_____

How **Setting** is used: _____

_____

Why it's important: _____

_____

How **Theme** is used: _____

_____

Why it's important: _____

_____

Finish this first paragraph by stating which element you feel most makes the novel unique, interesting, or entertaining.

AN ELEMENTAL CHOICE (CONT.)

Paragraph 2 — Use this paragraph to support and defend the claim you made at the end of Paragraph 1. Provide three examples from the novel that show why this element contributes so greatly to the success of the novel.

	Example	**How It Contributes**
1.		
2.		
3.		

Paragraph 3 — Restate your opinion and wrap up your essay.

_____

_____

_____

After you have completed this outline, write a rough draft of your essay on a separate piece of paper. Use the checklist below to make sure your essay has everything that is required.

SELF-EDITING CHECKLIST

Check off the box next to each item once you have included that element in your essay.

- ❏ I have introduced the terms *voice*, *plot*, *setting*, and *theme*.

- ❏ I have stated why each element is important to the novel.

- ❏ I have stated which element is most responsible for making the novel successful.

- ❏ I have given at least three examples that support my opinion.

- ❏ I have restated my opinion and concluded my essay.

- ❏ Throughout my essay, I used transition words to move from one example or paragraph to the next.

- ❏ I have checked my essay for spelling, punctuation, and grammar mistakes.

A NOVEL POSTER
TEACHER INSTRUCTIONS

This activity offers students an opportunity to demonstrate understanding of the novel by creating visual representations of its parts.

Materials Required: poster board, markers

Optional Materials: scissors, glue, magazines, Internet access, sticky notes

✦ To begin, divide the class into groups of students. The ideal number in each group is 5, but smaller or larger groups will also be possible.

✦ Next, assign a chapter or section from the novel to each group. Choose from the list to the right.

✦ Distribute the student page (page 71). Have students read the instructions for what to include on their posters.

✦ Give students plenty of time to plan and create their posters. If you wish, allow them to access magazines or the Internet so they may search for appropriate images to include.

✦ After groups have completed their posters, hang the posters around the room. Conduct a gallery walk.

Chapter 2
Chapter 3
Chapter 6
Chapter 8
Chapter 11
Chapter 14
Chapter 16
Chapter 18

Ideas for a Gallery Walk

Allow students to move around the room and examine each poster. Equip students with sticky notes. When they have questions regarding another group's poster, they can write their questions on sticky notes and attach these notes directly to the poster. Guide your students to think about the following ideas as they prepare to ask questions:

✓ Is an idea on the poster not clear?

✓ Do you disagree with a point the poster makes?

✓ Do you want more information about something the group has included?

✓ Do you want to ask how the group felt about any particular scene or character?

✓ Do you want to bring up something you thought was important in that chapter but isn't included on the poster?

Once students have completed this process, allow groups to answer the question(s) attached to their posters.

A NOVEL POSTER (CONT.)
STUDENT INSTRUCTIONS

Your group will work together to create a poster that represents one chapter from *Bud, Not Buddy*. Your group will present this poster to the class. Each person will be responsible for explaining one part of the poster.

> **Our group has been assigned Chapter _____.**

Talk about the events in your chapter and decide which one is the most important.

Your poster should contain all of the elements below. Write down who will be in charge of each one.

#	Elements	Assigned to
1	• the number of the chapter • a short (no more than three sentences) explanation of what happens in this chapter	
2	• the name(s) of the characters in the chapter • a short explanation or diagram showing why these characters are in this part of the novel together	
3	• images representing the most important event in this scene • an explanation of why this event is so important	
4	• a quotation from this section • explanation of the significance of the quotation	
5	• a few words that represent the feeling or mood of this chapter • an explanation of why this mood is appropriate in this chapter	

Tips for Making Posters

✦ **Be creative!** You may draw pictures, use pictures from magazines, print images from the Internet (with permission from your teacher), or paste on objects that relate to the story.

✦ **Plan before you start.** Everyone should collect their pictures and ideas before anyone begins writing on the poster board. Work together to design the look of the poster by placing all pictures before you paste them. Don't forget to leave room for the written parts.

NAME: _____

A PERSUASIVE LETTER

Imagine a school in another town is considering using *Bud, Not Buddy* in its classrooms. First, they want your thoughts on the novel.

Write a letter to the principal of this imaginary school. Give your opinion of the book and explain why it should be taught there or why it should not.

Follow this outline, and then write your letter on a separate piece of paper.

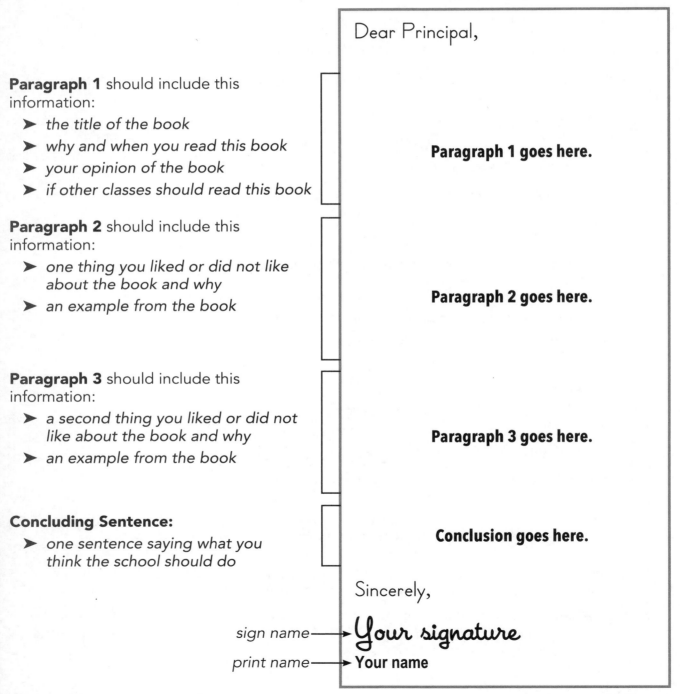

Paragraph 1 should include this information:
- ➤ *the title of the book*
- ➤ *why and when you read this book*
- ➤ *your opinion of the book*
- ➤ *if other classes should read this book*

Paragraph 2 should include this information:
- ➤ *one thing you liked or did not like about the book and why*
- ➤ *an example from the book*

Paragraph 3 should include this information:
- ➤ *a second thing you liked or did not like about the book and why*
- ➤ *an example from the book*

Concluding Sentence:
- ➤ *one sentence saying what you think the school should do*

Dear Principal,

Paragraph 1 goes here.

Paragraph 2 goes here.

Paragraph 3 goes here.

Conclusion goes here.

Sincerely,

sign name ——➤ *Your signature*

print name ——➤ **Your name**

NAME: _____

MY BOOK RATING

What did you like or dislike about the book? Think about the story elements and rank each one. Use the following rating scale.

0 stars	1 star	2 stars	3 stars	4 stars	5 stars
☆☆☆☆☆	★☆☆☆☆	★★☆☆☆	★★★☆☆	★★★★☆	★★★★★
terrible	bad	okay	good	great	amazing!

Characters ☆☆☆☆☆

Reason: _____

_____

Setting ☆☆☆☆☆

Reason: _____

_____

Point of View ☆☆☆☆☆

Reason: _____

_____

Plot ☆☆☆☆☆

Reason: _____

_____

The Ending ☆☆☆☆☆

Reason: _____

_____

Themes ☆☆☆☆☆

Reason: _____

_____

Overall, I give this book _____ stars because _____

_____

_____

TEACHER INSTRUCTIONS

The novel *Bud, Not Buddy* contains vocabulary that is integral to the novel's plot, characters, and themes. Christopher Paul Curtis's word choices play an important role in establishing the voices of the characters, creating the mood of the story, and revealing the time period in which the story is set.

On page 75 is a list of the most challenging and important vocabulary words in *Bud, Not Buddy*. These words are listed in the order in which they appear in the novel. The chapter in which the word can be found is listed in parentheses after each word.

Select words from these section lists to assign for the "Choice Words" Interactive Novel Log entries (see page 18).

Other Ideas for Assigning Vocabulary

✦ **Traditional Vocabulary Lesson** — Select a total of 10 to 20 words for the entire class to study and learn.

✦ **Personalized Vocabulary** — Post the lists in the classroom and allow students to select their own word(s) to study.

✦ **Students as Teachers** — For each section, assign a different word to pairs or groups of students. Have the members of each group do a short presentation on their word's meaning and usage.

After your students have finished reading the entire novel, review vocabulary from each section by using one or more of the following activities.

✦ **Create a crossword puzzle.** Use at least one vocabulary word from each section of the novel.

✦ **Design an illustrated dictionary.** Choose 10 or more words from the novel. Draw pictures to depict those words.

✦ **Write a poem.** Use at least one vocabulary word from each section of the novel.

✦ **Play a Jeopardy!-style game.** Make a game board with definitions of vocabulary words. Students or student groups compete to identify the correct words.

This adjective means "all right" or "satisfactory."	What is **copacetic**?

✦ **Hold a vocabulary-in-context contest!** Have students write short stories that properly use as many vocabulary words as possible. Select a few stories with the highest number of vocabulary words used, read them aloud to the class, and have the class vote for the story that makes the best use of vocabulary words.

NOVEL VOCABULARY

For each word, the chapter number is given in parentheses. The words can be found in the novel in the order in which they are shown here.

Section I	Section II	Section III	Section IV	Section V
temporary (1)	fumbling (5)	pictorial (9)	scamp (13)	sympathy (16)
foster (1)	privilege (6)	devoured (9)	palest (13)	wiry (16)
depression (1)	considerate (6)	ignorant (9)	festering (13)	copacetic (16)
commence (1)	drowsy (7)	terminally (9)	shunned (13)	ratty (16)
decoder (1)	hypnotizing (7)	warblers (9)	kin (13)	fitting (16)
S.R.O. (1)	retrieve (7)	boisterous (9)	meddling (13)	embouchure (16)
suspicion (1)	matrimonial (7)	rustle (10)	prying (13)	senior (16)
luxurious (1)	radiating (7)	definite (10)	reserved (14)	nominate (16)
welted (2)	thumbed (7)	ventriloquists (10)	acquaintance (14)	compromise (16)
blubbery (2)	gait (7)	slew (11)	stampede (14)	musings (16)
urchins (2)	hoodlum (8)	slogging (11)	grouchy (14)	prodigy (16)
sputtered (2)	criminal (8)	paltry (11)	impression (14)	squabs (17)
ingratitude (2)	fidgeting (8)	reputation (11)	snooping (15)	slacking (17)
uplifted (2)		scolding (11)	contaminated (15)	interrupt (17)
conscience (2)		knickers (11)		offended (18)
plagues (2)		worrisome (11)		practical (18)
vermin (2)		lick (11)		stiffed (18)
assurance (2)		flimsy (12)		nudging (18)
rafters (3)		resourceful (12)		bearer (18)
tussling (3)		alias (12)		rummaging (18)
lam (4)		loathsome (12)		ornery (19)
		confidential (12)		
		negotiating (12)		
		sully (12)		
		moldering (12)		

ANSWER KEY

For many of the questions in this resource, answers will vary and will be subject to interpretation. Accept student work that responds appropriately to the questions asked and provides evidence from the text when called for. Refer to the answers listed below when more specific responses may be needed.

+ +

"And the Winner Was . . ." (page 8)

Newbery Medal: named after John Newbery, an 18th-century English publisher of children's books; first given in 1922 to the author of the "most distinguished contribution to American literature for children"; looks like a gold medal (circle) with an open book in the middle and the words "John Newbery Medal" around the top; *Bud, Not Buddy* won in 2000.

Coretta Scott King Book Award: named after Coretta Scott King, a civil rights leader and also the wife of Dr. Martin Luther King Jr.; first given in 1970 to African American authors and illustrators who create books for young readers; looks like a bronze circle overlapped by a bronze pyramid that features a reader, an open book, and several small symbols; *Bud, Not Buddy* won in 2000.

"Rules and Things" (page 13)

Student signs should read: "Bud Caldwell's Rules and Things for Having a Funner Life and Making a Better Liar Out of Yourself"

"In the Beginning" (page 21)

1. "Here we go again."

2. *Bud's age:* 10. *Bud's Present:* He is told that he is leaving the orphanage to go live with a foster family. He carries around a suitcase that contains flyers about a jazz band. He thinks the band leader is his father. *Bud's Past:* He has been living at an orphanage. His mother died when he was six. He has lived with two foster families previously. The first foster family beat him up at times. *Bud's Future:* He will be going to live with the Amos family. The family includes a 12-year-old boy.

3. "Here we go again." This line begins the novel, and it is also repeated halfway through Chapter 1.

"Getting to Know Bud" (page 22)

1. *Possible answers:* his suitcase, the blue flyer in his suitcase, not letting someone take advantage of him, doing what is necessary to survive and to protect himself, understanding why people do the things they do.

2. Accept appropriate responses. Students may say that he does what he needs to do to protect himself. Sometimes that means that he stands up for himself and fights. Other times, that means that he lies and/or pretends to think something other than what he really thinks.

3–4. Accept appropriate responses.

"The Last Laugh" (page 24)

1. Answers may vary. First, he wants to find the shotgun and hide it so it can't be used against him. Next, he wants to find his suitcase and put it where he can grab it quickly and run. Then, he plans to fill up a glass with warm water. After that, he plans to put Todd's finger in the water, because he thinks that will make Todd wet the bed.

2. He can't get Todd to wet his bed. Instead, he just pours the water over Todd and "wets" the bed for him.

3. The plan will help him get revenge on Todd because it will embarrass Todd and also get him in trouble with his mother for wetting the bed. The plan will help him get revenge on Mrs. Amos because it will get her mattress wet and also make her angry at her son.

4. "He who laughs last laughs best."

5. Accept appropriate responses.

"Things About Momma" (page 28)

1. "Everything moved very, very fast when Momma was near, she was like a tornado, never resting, always looking around us, never standing still."

2. She would squeeze his arms, hold him steady, and look him in the eyes.

3. Four things: the picture; Bud's name; she would explain things to him when he was older; the idea that when one door closes, another opens. Accept appropriate responses for the "Details" column.

4. Accept appropriate responses.

"The Pretend Family" (page 30)

1. He is angry with Bud, because Bud is trying to get in the food line that is already closed. He says kids these days talk too much and don't listen. He threatens to beat Bud with a strap.

2. Clarence is Bud. That is the name the tall man calls him. Bud's first reaction is to tell the man that his name isn't Clarence.

3. He is firm with Bud and slaps him on the back of the head. After that, he laughs around Bud and is kind.

4. When the other man is looking, she is firm with Bud and slaps him a bit to show him that she is not happy with his actions. Once that man is no longer around, she is kind to Bud and even gives him brown sugar for his breakfast.

5. Accept appropriate responses. Students should note that Mr. Amos didn't want to be bothered, while the pretend father took control of the situation and helped Bud. Mrs. Amos lectured Bud and assumed he was bad, while the pretend mother was kind and generous to Bud and assumed he was good. Todd Amos physically assaulted Bud, while the pretend brother just made fun of him a bit and stuck out his tongue at Bud.

ANSWER KEY (CONT.)

"Signs of the Times" (page 31)

Sign Outside the Mission: Students should draw a family of four in a car. The people in the family should all look the same, except the parents are bigger. The sign reads "There's No Place Like America Today!"

Signs Inside the Mission: Students should quote two of the signs mentioned in Chapter 6.

"A Sense of Place" (page 32)

Accept appropriate responses. Students should first correctly identify that Chapter 7 mostly takes place in a library, while Chapter 8 mostly takes place in a "Hooverville" (a makeshift town).

"A Night in Hooverville" (page 33)

1. Accept appropriate responses. The town was made up of cardboard huts and shacks. People who don't have a home or are on their way somewhere else live there.

2. Accept any order. One fire is very large, and there are 100 people sitting in a circle around it cooking or eating food. Another fire is smaller, and it has a large pot on it. Someone with a large stick is stirring the pot in order to wash the clothes inside. The third fire is very small. There is a white family with a sick baby sitting around it.

3. It's named after President Herbert Hoover, who the people blame for their troubles.

4. Answers may vary. Bud talks to people, eats a delicious meal, is put on "KP" ("Kitchen Patrol"), shares a kiss with Deza Malone, has trouble sleeping, thinks about his mother, and has a strange dream.

5. Answers may vary. Bud wakes up to a man yelling that the train is leaving. Everyone starts running for the train. He almost loses the blue flyer twice. Policemen try to keep the people from jumping the train. Bugs gets on the train, but Bud doesn't make it. Cops burn down the Hooverville and kick everyone out.

"A Growing Idea" (page 36)

1. He compares his idea to a seed that starts out very small but grows into a large tree.

2. Accept appropriate responses. Possible stages: Bud's mother brings home a band flyer; a bully teases Bud about not having a father, which causes Bud to blurt out that Herman E. Calloway is his father; Bud begins to feel that his mother must be leaving the flyers and rocks as clues.

Considering Setting: The last two flyers claim the bands are from Poland (Warsaw) and Germany (Berlin). These are European cities, and people of that time would not expect the band members to be African American. Some people might not hire the band if they knew what they looked like.

"The Road to Grand Rapids" (page 37)

1. The distance is 120 miles. Earlier, the librarian told him that he could walk about 5 miles per hour. Students should show this equation: 120 miles ÷ 5 mph = 24 hours.

2. Students should write four of the following: Owasso, Ovid, St. John's, Ionia, Lowell.

3. *City:* road – paved; sign – "You Are Now Leaving Flint, Hurry Back"; sounds – honking cars, shifting gears, people yelling
Country: road – dirt; sign – "You Are Now Entering Flint – Enjoy Your Stay"; sounds – insects and animals making noise, moving around, eating and getting eaten

4. *Place:* Owosso, Michigan. *Time:* 2:30 in the morning

Research It: a. 25, b. 5

"They Have Their Reasons" (page 38)

1. He doesn't think it's safe for a "brown-skinned boy" to be walking alone at night in that part of the country.

2. He wants a sandwich and some red pop.

3. He thinks it's very dangerous. Many of the people of Owosso don't want black people in their town.

4. Bud thinks the man is a vampire. The man has a box of human blood in his car.

5. For one, he has a job to do, and he has to get this blood to someone who needs it. For another, he feels it's not safe for him to be in Owosso and harm could come to him.

"A Different Kind of Home" (page 39)

1. He learns the following things: they took off his knickers; everyone in Grand Rapids knows Herman E. Calloway; Herman was married at least one other time; Herman has at least one other child, but she is an adult; Herman has a reputation for being no-nonsense but not mean.

2.

Character's Name	Relationship to Others
Lefty Lewis	father to Mrs. Sleet; grandfather to Kim and Scott
Mrs. Sleet	daughter of Lefty; mother to Kim and Scott
Kim	granddaughter of Lefty; daughter of Mrs. Sleet; sister to Scott
Scott	grandson of Lefty; son of Mrs. Sleet; brother to Kim

3. The family teases each other a lot. They are silly with each other. They eat a lot of food, some of which Bud has never had before. They talk a lot while they eat, and they seem to enjoy each other's company. Bud has never been around a family that were so free and easy with each other.

4. Answers may vary. Students may say that the two families are similar in that they seem to be close. They are very different in that one struggles for food, while the other has an abundance of it. Also, Lefty's family talks freely a lot, while the pretend family must be quiet and not bring attention to themselves.

ANSWER KEY (CONT.)

"On the Road" (page 40)

1. The policeman is stopping any car he doesn't recognize, because there has been news that labor organizers are in Flint from Detroit.

2. a. *What Is Really Happening:* A policeman pulls over Lefty's car. Lefty acts like he has something to hide. Lefty asks Bud to hide a box. *What Bud Thinks Is Happening:* The FBI has caught up with him. Lefty might be on the lam, too. Lefty has a gun in the box and is ready to shoot it out with the policeman.

3. Each letter costs money, so a telegram must have very few letters. Only important information is given. One writes the word "STOP" in place of a period.

"The Old Man" (page 41)

1. He becomes worried, and his heart starts beating fast.

2. He tells him that he is embarrassed, and he wants to see his father first. Lefty agrees as long as he holds onto Bud's suitcase to be sure Bud doesn't run away.

3. a. Herman talks and tells stories just like Bud. He even says the exact same thing that Bud thought earlier (about when it's the right time to say you've had enough).
   b. Herman is much older than Bud thought he would be.

"Player Cards" (page 44)

Band members: Herman E. Calloway, none, bass fiddle; Jimmy Wesley, Mr. Jimmy, horn; Doug Tennant, the Thug, drums; Harrison Eddie Patrick, Steady Eddie, saxophone; Chug Cross, Doo-Doo Bug, trombone; Roy Breed, Dirty Deed, piano; Grace Thomas, none, vocal stylist (singer)

"Say What They Mean" (page 45)

Phrase #1: Steady Eddie, "Be careful with that instrument because it is what I use to make my money."
Phrase #2: Herman Calloway, "This is your idea, so you take responsibility for it and don't involve me."
Phrase #3: Steady Eddie, "You should leave the kid alone and not make fun of him so much."
Phrase #4: Steady Eddie, "The person in the front seat probably won't have his drumming job for very much longer."

"Home Cooking" (page 46)

Students should mention some or all of the following: Steady Eddie's sense of humor, Miss Thomas's kindness, the sound of Miss Thomas's humming, the happiness of the crowd in the restaurant, the smells in the restaurant.

"A Night at the Station" (page 47)

1. Grand Calloway Station

2. It's named after Grand Central Station, because just like that place, a lot of people go in and out of Herman's house.

3. It is a little girl's room. There is a bed, a dresser, and a lamp with a horse on it. Two little doors lead to a closet.

4. He thinks this because Miss Thomas tells him that the girl whose room it was is gone. Bud thinks that when adults use the word *gone* to describe someone, they really mean "dead."

5. The door next to Bud's is Miss Thomas's. The next one is Herman's. The door across the hall is the bathroom.

6. Miss Thomas is asking Herman to lock the closet doors in Bud's room, and he is angry and doesn't want to do it. We know this because Bud asks Miss Thomas if the doors are locked and because Herman comes back into the room and angrily locks them.

"The Decision" (page 50)

1. Bud will stay with the band for a while and travel with them.

2. Accept appropriate quotes.

3. He must be patient with them, because they don't usually have children around. He must be clean and do his fair share of the chores.

4. He gives him a new suitcase to put his belongings in. He also gives him an instrument to learn to use to play music.

"Part of the Band" (page 51)

1. They say he needs a nickname. This shows acceptance, because they all have nicknames by which they call each other.

2. She thinks this nickname stuff is silly, and she has no interest in being a part of it.

3. Sleepy LaBone

4. "Sleepy" is because he slept so late that morning. "Bone" is because he's so skinny. They made the last name "LaBone," because it sounds French and classy.

5. He loves it.

"What We Learn" (page 53)

1. He says that Herman needs a white person in the band.

2. Herman can't own property in the area where Grand Calloway Station is located, and so it is in Dirty Deed's name. Also, Dirty Deed negotiates for the band so that club owners think they are booking an all-white band. By the time the band shows up, it is too late to cancel. These two examples show how characters are affected by the time period in which the novel is set (America in the 1930s).

3. Herman stays back to talk to an old friend, and Bud stays back to load the equipment.

4. He finds a good throwing rock and asks Bud to pick it up.

5. He finds lots of rocks with places and dates written on them.

6. First, Herman found a rock and picked it up. Next, Herman wrote on it. Then, he gave the rock to his daughter. Finally, she gave the rock to Bud, her son.

"Historical Figures" (page 65)

Said/Thought by Bud: John Dillinger, J. Edgar Hoover, Pretty Boy Floyd, Baby Face Nelson, Machine Gun Kelly
Said By Another Character: President Herbert Hoover (mouth-organ man), Ruth Dandridge (Lefty Lewis), George Washington Carver (Lefty Lewis), John Brown (Lefty Lewis), Blind Lemon Jefferson (Miss Thomas)

MEETING STANDARDS

The lessons and activities included in *Rigorous Reading: An In-Depth Guide for Bud, Not Buddy* meet the following Common Core State Standards for grades 4–6. (©Copyright 2010. National Governors Association Center for Best Practices and Council of Chief State School Officers. All rights reserved.)

The code for each standard covered in this resource is listed in the table below and on page 80. The codes are listed in boldface, and the page numbers of the activities that meet that standard are listed in regular type. For more information about the Common Core State Standards and for a full listing of the descriptions associated with each code, go to *http://www.corestandards.org/ or visit http://www.teachercreated.com/standards/*.

Here is an example of an English Language Arts (ELA) code and how to read it:

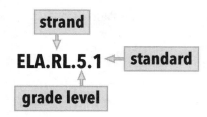

ELA Strands
L = Language
W = Writing
RF = Reading: Foundational Skills
RL = Reading: Literature
SL = Speaking and Listening

+ +

Strand Reading: Literature	**Substrand** Key Ideas and Details

ELA.RL.4.1, ELA.RL.6.1: 11–55, 57–69, 71–73

ELA.RL.5.1: 12–14, 18, 20–21, 24, 27–29, 31, 35–38, 41, 43, 49, 51–52, 57–59, 71

ELA.RL.4.2, ELA.RL.5.2, ELA.RL.6.2: 11–17, 20–22, 25, 27–31, 33, 35–36, 38–41, 43, 46–47, 49–54, 57–61, 63–69, 71–72

ELA.RL.4.3: 11–17, 20–25, 27–41, 43–47, 49–54, 57–69, 71

ELA.RL.5.3: 12, 15–17, 20–22, 27–28, 30–33, 35–39, 43, 48–52, 54, 60, 64–65, 67–69

ELA.RL.6.3: 11–17, 20–25, 27–33, 35–36, 38–41, 43, 46–47, 49–51, 53–54, 57–66, 68–69, 71

Strand Reading: Literature	**Substrand** Craft and Structure

ELA.RL.4.4, ELA.RL.5.4, ELA.RL.6.4: 11–55, 57–69, 71–73, 75

ELA.RL.5.5, ELA.RL.6.5: 11–13, 15–16, 18–21, 23–25, 27–28, 30–33, 35–36, 38–41, 43, 45–47, 49–54, 57–65, 68–69, 71

ELA.RL.4.6: 17, 20, 27, 35, 43, 49, 62

ELA.RL.5.6: 12, 15–17, 20–25, 27–33, 35–36, 38–41, 43, 46–47, 49–54, 57–59, 62–69

ELA.RL.6.6: 11–16, 20–25, 27–33, 35–36, 38–41, 43, 46–47, 49–51, 53–54, 57–59, 62, 64–69

Strand Reading: Literature	**Substrand** Range of Reading and Level of Text Complexity

ELA.RL.4.10, ELA.RL.5.10, ELA.RL.6.10: 11–55, 57–69, 71–73, 75

+ +

Strand Reading: Foundational Skills	**Substrand** Phonics and Word Recognition

ELA.RF.4.3, ELA.RF.5.3: 8–9, 11–55, 57–69, 71–73, 75

Strand Reading: Foundational Skills	**Substrand** Fluency

ELA.RF.4.4, ELA.RF.5.4: 8–9, 11–55, 57–69, 71–73, 75

MEETING STANDARDS (CONT.)

+ +

Strand Writing   **Substrand** Text Types and Purposes

ELA.W.4.1, ELA.W.5.1, ELA.W.6.1: 9, 11–13, 15–17, 19–36, 39, 42–44, 46, 48–49, 52, 54–55, 57–62, 64–65, 67–69, 72–73

ELA.W.4.2, ELA.W.5.2, ELA.W.6.2: 8–9, 11–55, 57–62, 64–69, 72

ELA.W.4.3, ELA.W.5.3, ELA.W.6.3: 17, 20, 26–27, 34–35, 40, 43, 48–49, 55, 60, 62–63, 66–67

Strand Writing   **Substrand** Production and Distribution of Writing

ELA.W.4.4, ELA.W.5.4, ELA.W.6.4: 8–9, 11–55, 57–69, 71–73, 75

ELA.W.4.5, ELA.W.5.5, ELA.W.6.5: 63, 68–69, 72

Strand Writing   **Substrand** Research to Build and Present Knowledge

ELA.W.4.7, ELA.W.5.7, ELA.W.6.7: 8, 36–37, 65

ELA.W.4.8, ELA.W.5.8, ELA.W.6.8: 9, 16–20, 25–27, 31–36, 38–39, 42–43, 48–49, 55, 57–59, 65–69, 72

ELA.W.4.9, ELA.W.5.9, ELA.W.6.9: 8–9, 11–55, 57–69, 71–73, 75

Strand Writing   **Substrand** Range of Writing

ELA.W.4.10, ELA.W.5.10, ELA.W.6.10: 8–9, 11–55, 57–69, 71–73, 75

+ +

Strand Speaking and Listening   **Substrand** Comprehension and Collaboration

ELA.SL.4.1, ELA.SL.5.1, ELA.SL.6.1: 25, 32, 39, 44–45, 54, 63, 71

ELA.SL.4.2, ELA.SL.5.2, ELA.SL.6.2: 25, 54

ELA.SL.4.3, ELA.SL.5.3, ELA.SL.6.3: 25, 32, 39, 54

Strand Speaking and Listening   **Substrand** Presentation of Knowledge and Ideas

ELA.SL.4.4, ELA.SL.5.4, ELA.SL.6.4: 25, 32, 54, 63, 71

ELA.SL.4.5, ELA.SL.5.5, ELA.SL.6.5: 70–71

ELA.SL.4.6, ELA.SL.5.6, ELA.SL.6.6: 63, 71

+ +

Strand Language   **Substrand** Conventions of Standard English

ELA.L.4.1, ELA.L.5.1, ELA.L.6.1: 8–9, 11–55, 56–73, 75

ELA.L.4.2, ELA.L.5.2, ELA.L.6.2: 8–9, 11–55, 56–73, 75

Strand Language   **Substrand** Knowledge of Language

ELA.L.4.3, ELA.L.5.3, ELA.L.6.3: 8–9, 11–55, 56–73, 75

Strand Language   **Substrand** Vocabulary Acquisition and Use

ELA.L.4.4, ELA.L.5.4, ELA.L.6.4: 8–9, 11–55, 56–73, 75

ELA.L.4.5, ELA.L.5.5, ELA.L.6.5: 8–9, 11–55, 56–73, 75

ELA.L.4.6, ELA.L.5.6, ELA.L.6.6: 8–9, 11–55, 56–73, 75